THE COMMONWEALTH AND INTERNATIONAL LIBRARY

*Joint Chairmen of the Honorary Editorial Advisory Board*

SIR ROBERT ROBINSON, O.M., F.R.S., LONDON

DEAN ATHELSTAN SPILHAUS, MINNESOTA

*Publisher:* ROBERT MAXWELL, M.C., M.P.

SOCIOLOGY DIVISION

*General Editor:* A. H. RICHMOND

# An Introduction to Sociology

# An Introduction to Sociology

BY

**BRYAN S. R. GREEN**, B.A., M.A. (Illinois), Ph.D.
*Lecturer in Sociology, School of Humanities and
Social Sciences, Bath University of Technology*

AND

**EDWARD A. JOHNS**, B.Sc. (Econ), A.C.C.S., A.M.B.I.M.
*Senior Lecturer in Industrial Sociology,
Department of Management, Slough College of Technology*

1966
THE QUEEN'S AWARD
TO INDUSTRY 1966

**PERGAMON PRESS**
OXFORD · LONDON · EDINBURGH · NEW YORK
TORONTO · SYDNEY · PARIS · BRAUNSCHWEIG

Pergamon Press Ltd., Headington Hill Hall, Oxford
4 & 5 Fitzroy Square, London W.1
Pergamon Press (Scotland) Ltd., 2 & 3 Teviot Place, Edinburgh 1
Pergamon Press Inc., 44–01 21st Street, Long Island City, New York 11101
Pergamon of Canada Ltd., 207 Queen's Quay West, Toronto 1
Pergamon Press (Aust.) Pty. Ltd., 19a Boundary Street,
Rushcutters Bay, N.S.W. 2011
Pergamon Press S.A.R.L., 24 rue des Écoles, Paris 5[e]
Vieweg & Sohn GmbH, Burgplatz 1, Braunschweig

Copyright © 1966 Pergamon Press Ltd.
First edition 1966
Reprinted 1968
Library of Congress Catalog Card No. 66-26869

*Printed in Great Britain by A Wheaton & Co., Exeter*

.

08 012154 3 (flexicover)
08 012155 1 (hard cover)

# CONTENTS

# INTRODUCTION

As SOCIAL scientists have accumulated knowledge concerning the behaviour of human beings in society, so they have become increasingly reluctant to make broad generalizations. In contemporary sociology the essence of sophistication is *qualification*. The impression of certainty which is conveyed in an introductory textbook is a product of the need for conciseness and for the provision of stable reference points to someone just entering the subject. The erosion of certainty is a matter for later development when tolerance of ambiguity may be higher.

Many introductory textbooks take the student upon a conducted tour of the whole extensive field of sociological study. In a short book such an encyclopaedic approach is impossible and will not be attempted here. The intention is to introduce the student to the theoretical approaches, the methods of inquiry and the concepts with which sociologists attempt to order the complex phenomena of social interaction. In doing this we shall make reference to past attempts in this direction, i.e. to the development of sociology as well as some current ones. Illustrations of specific investigations will be given which may provide some insights into substantive aspects of society and social behaviour, but the main concern is with how sociologists go about their work rather than with what they have discovered. Sociology cannot be defined in terms of its subject matter, its terminology, or of its methods alone, but only through a combination of these things; they form the three major topics around which the book is organized.

# CHAPTER 1

# SOCIOLOGY AS A SCIENTIFIC DISCIPLINE

ONE of the most puzzling and irritating aspects of sociology to someone first exposed to it is the contrast between the subject matter, which consists largely of aspects of social existence familiar to the layman, and the language used by the sociologist in analysing and describing it; this being largely unfamiliar, esoteric and "technical". Part of the difficulty in accepting the necessity of such a language lies in the fact that we are social beings already possessing an everyday language which we use to order our own lives and to make sense of the social world around us. It is hoped that this chapter will show why special words, or the special use of familiar words, is necessary.

It is the aspiration of sociology to be a scientific discipline which sets the sociologist apart from the social philosopher, the social critic and the journalistic commentator, even though they may be concerned with the same phenomena. This is not to say that the sociologist claims a monopoly of knowledge or understanding regarding society. He is merely developing one approach to further understanding as intensively as possible. If the results ultimately prove less enlightening than those produced by the philosopher, the commentator or the novelist then at least it can be argued that the effort to apply the methods of scientific explanation to social data was necessary and worth while.

The most general aim of a science is to establish empirically validated propositions (sometimes called "laws") concerning the relationships between events and objects which can be observed directly or indirectly. The scientific approach in social studies may

1

at first sight appear desiccated and dull compared to the vivid descriptions possible in historical narrative or to the exciting speculations possible in social philosophy. However, it must be understood that science is first and foremost an intellectual discipline with certain methods of procedure and requirements of proof peculiar to itself. The concern of the sociologist, as a scientist, is to introduce theoretical order into the complexity of social life.

One of the hallmarks of the scientist is that he seeks to explain a particular event or observation as a logical deduction from a general proposition or set of propositions. In the present unsophisticated stage of theoretical development in sociology this ideal is not often attainable and the sociologist more often uses observations to illustrate general propositions or suggest hypotheses. Nonetheless the ideal is still there. This aspect of scientific explanation may be clarified by taking a specific social phenomenon, the French Revolution of 1789, and illustrating the difference between a historical and a sociological explanation of it.

In historical explanation an attempt is made to reconstruct the chain of events leading up to this unique happening; the focus is upon specific individuals and groups reacting to particular social, economic and political conditions. The aim of the historian in this case would be an accurate reconstruction of the French Revolution and the events leading up to it. For the sociologist this end product would be used for constructing and testing general propositions concerning revolution. For example, James C. Davies in a recent article uses this and other revolutions to suggest certain hypotheses.[1] One of them states that revolutions are most likely to occur where a prolonged period of general social and economic improvement is followed by a short period of sharp regression. The long period of improvement generates an increasing number of wants and perceived needs in the population together with an increased expectation that these will be satisfied. The sharp reversal in what people actually get leaves an

[1] James C. Davies, Toward a theory of revolution, *American Sociological Review*, **27** (Feb. 1962), 5.

intolerable gap between actual need satisfaction and expected need satisfaction. This gap is manifested, psychologically, as anxiety, frustration and aggression and, politically, as a revolutionary situation. It is the state of mind rather than the objective level of socio-economic welfare which produces revolution. Persons who differ greatly in outward signs of well-being may be equal in the frustration and aggression they feel and so become revolutionary allies.

Although these ideas are useful as research guides and as means for drawing together a wide variety of historical information they do not constitute a proper theory of revolution.

In order to understand why not, it is necessary to go into the question of what constitutes a scientific theory. In doing so we shall utilize R. B. Braithwaite's excellent discussion of the logic of scientific inquiry.[1]

Braithwaite defines a scientific theory in a strict sense as a set of propositions taking the form of a deductive system, i.e. there are initial assumptions and general propositions from which further propositions of increasing specificity are derived according to logical principles. The most specific or lowest-level propositions are the working hypotheses which are tested by observation. It is by confirming or refuting these that we test the empirical validity of the whole logical structure of propositions, i.e. the theory. When an empirical hypothesis (one testable by experience) is held to be true at any level of generality, then we have what is called a scientific "law". This term is used with some hesitation because it implies a degree of certainty which not even the natural sciences now claim.

Going a step further we may define a scientific proposition as the statement of a relationship between specified properties of objects and events. This implies not merely that a relationship exists, but that some specification of the relationship is possible, e.g. a prediction of what will happen to one property if there is a change in another.

[1] R. B. Braithwaite, *Scientific Explanation*, Cambridge University Press, 1953.

The propositions of Davies concerning revolution are not linked in the form of a deductive system, neither do they specify the values of the relevant variables by which one could predict that revolution will occur. In fairness to Davies, it should be emphasized that he attempted only to prepare the way for a general theory and made no claims actually to have formulated one.

In the strict sense of the word there are few general theories in sociology, although there are many abstract concepts, hypotheses and empirical observations. One of the few examples of a general theory in sociology is provided by Emile Durkheim's study of suicide rates.[1] It should be emphasized that this is a theory of suicide *rates* and not an explanation of suicide at the individual level. As elaborated by Robert K. Merton,[2] the propositions constituting the theory are as follows:

1. Social cohesion provides psychological support to persons subjected to stress and anxiety.
2. Suicide rates are functions of unrelieved stress and anxiety.
3. Specified social groupings have a higher degree of social cohesion than others (e.g. Catholics compared to Protestants)
4. Therefore, suicide rates will be lower among Catholics than Protestants.

The fourth proposition is merely one of many lower-order propositions or working hypotheses which could be derived from the others. In practice one would test as many of these as possible in order to expose the theory to a wide range of empirical evidence. The important thing is that the theory is *testable* by observation. Where theory is related directly to experience in this way there is the prospect of developing a cumulative programme of research as well as drawing together previously unrelated scraps of evidence. Sociologists have to formulate theories *and* provide empirical evidence in support of them.

A basic problem in testing propositions, whether these are

---

[1] E. Durkheim (trans. J. Spaulding and G. Simpson), *Suicide*, Free Press, 1951.

[2] Robert K. Merton, *Social Theory and Social Structure*, Free Press, 1957.

derived from a general theory or not, is that of relating abstract concepts and broad definitions to observation and experience. It is impossible, for example, directly to observe social cohesion. One has to construct observable indices to represent this abstract concept. Procedures for measuring or observing are termed *operational definitions*. At the simplest level of measurement an operational definition gives instructions on how to classify events or objects unambiguously. Many studies classify individuals according to "social class". One operational definition, used in the United Kingdom, instructs the researcher to establish the occupation of a person, then to look the occupation up in the Registrar-General's Classification of Occupations to see which of five prestige groupings it has been placed in. The general require-ment of an operational definition is to make it so precise that anyone else using it would obtain exactly the same results. It is important to note the essentially arbitrary relationship between operational and theoretical definitions. There is no logical way of proving that a given operational definition or index really refers to the underlying theoretical concept. It is a matter of argued plausibility and consensus of opinion. There may be more than one operational procedure which could be used to indicate a given concept. Some of these may be discarded through argument and the exposure of weaknesses, but there is always the possibility of being left with several indices of equal acceptability. If the use of different indices for the same concept produces different results then the researcher must conclude that the initial theoretical formulation of the concept was unsatisfactory and requires further refinement. One actually tests hypotheses in terms of the opera-tional definitions of concepts so that propositions involving abstract concepts are never *directly* testable. In sociology, as in politics and morality, the consequences of treating abstract ideas as though they were testable hypotheses is endless debate and fruitless argument.

Although the natural sciences are a model for scientific in-vestigation, this is not to deny that human interaction constitutes a rather special field of study. The social scientist, in his human capacity, can to some extent understand his subject matter from the inside, which is impossible for the natural scientist. This is most obvious in participant observation studies where the researcher actually becomes an actor in the situation he is studying and uses subjective understanding to interpret his data.[1] Some sociologists have been so impressed by the special qualities of their subject matter as to deny the validity of the methodology of the natural sciences in studying society. The differences of opinion between those with a "humanist" bias and those with a natural science bias have been exacerbated by emotional considerations. In the former case, there is a repugnance to the idea of treating human beings as though they were material objects to be observed in a spirit of scientific detachment. In the latter, there is a desire to achieve for sociology the status of a science and a certain impatience with the refined ambiguities of scholarly speculation. However, there is no inherent contradiction between subjective understanding and more rigorous scientific procedure. The former is a technique for gathering data which complements other means, such as the standardized questionnaire, the attitude scale or the analysis of official statistics. It is the task of the researcher to select the most appropriate techniques in terms of the questions he wishes to answer. In different cases it may be appropriate to read documents in a library, to live for several years in the same community, or to observe the behaviour of people in small groups under laboratory conditions. The important thing is not how one gathers the data, but adherence to the methodological rules of science in the setting up of propositions, the design of research and the interpretation of data.

## THEORETICAL CONCEPTS

We have already referred to operational definitions as an essential linking point between theory and research, but more needs to be said about the prior task of *developing theoretical concepts*.

---

[1] See, for example, W. F. Whyte, *Street Corner Society*, University of Chicago Press, 1943.

This is particularly important for someone just entering the field of "basic concepts" in introductory courses and textbooks. The initiate soon discovers that many concepts overlap in a confusing way and that he may be faced with learning two or more different definitions of the same word. This is particularly the case where definitions are made in a research vacuum, as in textbooks or in "pure" theory.

We can illustrate the point by considering three related concepts, viz. "role", "status" and "position", about which there is general agreement. All three terms must be defined in terms of a specific social system, e.g. a workgroup, an organization, a local community or a whole society. It is also agreed that their definition must include cultural elements, such as obligations, expectations or rules of conduct.

Harry M. Johnson, in one of the most widely used textbooks, defines a *social position* as something filled by an individual member of a social system.[1] The position consists of two main elements: (1) expectations and obligations held by other members concerning the behaviour of the *position incumbent*; (2) rights or the legitimate expectations of the position incumbent concerning the behaviour of other members. The first element Johnson calls the *role* of a position; the second element he calls the *status* of a position. This is, at least semantically, clear, but Johnson then goes on to note that the term "status" is sometimes used to denote the prestige of either a position or an individual. This, of course, is nearer the everyday usage of the word, and the confusion reflects the difficulty of transforming a familiar word into a technical term. Johnson says that the "apprentice sociologist" must learn to live with such inconsistencies and rely on the context to make sense of the word "status" in particular studies.

We have noted Johnson's definition of "role" to refer to duties attached to a position, but a more familiar definition in an equally popular textbook refers to "role" as the dynamic aspect of

[1] Harry M. Johnson, *Sociology: A Systematic Introduction*, New York, Harcourt, Brace & Co., 1960.

"status".[1] In this case, "status" refers to what Johnson calls "position" and "role" refers to the actual behaviour of a status incumbent, which Johnson and other writers call "role-perform-ance". Ely Chinoy, on the other hand, agrees with Davis in equating "status" with "position" (e.g. husband, foreman, soldier) but like Johnson uses "role" to refer to expectations and obligations.[2]

Apart from the waste of useful words which results from such duplication, there is a danger that the student, in an effort to avoid confusion, will be trapped into asking the unanswerable question, "what is the *real* meaning of a role or position or status?" This is to regress into the metaphysical search for essences which is the antithesis of scientific thought. The concept is a tool of research and the proper question is whether a given term, as defined *operationally*, is useful in accounting for observed phenomena or in linking empirical findings to higher order propositions. There is no reason why we should accept everyday usage as proof of the analytical utility of a term any more than we should reject familiar words on principle. Everyday terminology is particularly useful in descriptive studies, but the further one goes in the direction of analysis and the testing of propositions the greater the care that must be exercised in clarifying concepts.

One of the most fruitful means of conceptual clarification in sociology is the construction of typologies. The procedure is to take a commonly used concept such as leadership or job satisfaction and to analyse the elements which are implicit in the term or necessary to its definition. By the logical combination of these elements one forms a typology from what was a single concept. Quite often this enables one to reconcile previously contradictory findings as well as preparing the way for further research. Two illustrations of the procedure are given below, both of intrinsic interest.

The concept of conformity, as applied to individuals subjected to persuasion or pressure, is of central concern in such topics as

---

[1] Kingsly Davis, *Human Society*, New York, MacMillan, 1949.
[2] Ely Chinoy, *Sociological Perspectives*, Random House, 1954.

propaganda, advertising and brainwashing. An interesting attempt to clarify the concept so as to include the related concept of independence has been made by Marie Jahoda.[1] After a review of the literature, including a political case-study from John F. Kennedy's *Profiles in Courage* as well as research studies in social psychology, Jahoda distinguishes three elements necessary for a full definition of the concepts. These are: (a) whether the individual concerned has an intellectual or emotional investment in the issue; (b) whether the advocated position is adopted; (c) whether the individual's private opinion differs from his publicly expressed opinion. When these elements are dichotomized, i.e. divided into "yes"–"no" answers, there are eight possible combinations representing eight logically possible types of conformity-indepen-

| Investment in the issue | Yes | | | | No | | | |
|---|---|---|---|---|---|---|---|---|
| Adoption of advocated position | No | | Yes | | No | | Yes | |
| Private opinion differs from public | No | Yes | No | Yes | No | Yes | No | Yes |
| Types | a | b | c | d | e | f | g | h |

dence. Types (a) to (d) are similar in having an initial investment in the issue but differ in other ways. Type (a) refers to someone for whom the issue, say, the restriction of immigration in Britain, is salient and important but does not change his mind in the face of pressure or persuasion and feels at ease with himself on the matter. This could be called *independent dissent*. Type (b) still sticks to his opinion publicly but privately has changed his mind or has strong doubts. This would be called *undermined nonconformity*. Type (c) has changed his mind publicly and privately, this could be called *independent conformity*. Type (d) changes his mind publicly but not privately, this could be called *compliance*.

[1] Jahoda, Conformity and independence, *Human Relations* (Apr. 1959), p. 99.

Types (e) to (h) are similar in that the issue has no particular importance to them. Type (e) refuses to change his mind and feels no inner conflict about it. As the issue doesn't matter to him this is resistance to persuasion for its own sake and may be termed *compulsive non-conformity*. Type (f) is not empirically plausible, unless resistance is motivated by involvement in a related issue, say election to Parliament, and this would be called *expedient non-conformity*. Type (g) shows a change of position without any internal conflict and this may be termed *conformity*. Type (h) is similar to type (f) except that in this case one has *expedient conformity*.

If one accepts the typology in its general outlines then obviously it is necessary to formulate propositions in terms of specific types of conformity and non-conformity. This would help in making predictions from a practical point of view as well as contributing to research design and the construction of theory.

For another illustration of conceptual clarification we turn to a recent article by two British sociologists, which examines the concept of embourgeoisement.[1] This refers to the merging of the more prosperous sections of the working class into the middle class. The authors distinguish three elements which need to be considered if the concept is to be used as a basis for research:

(a) The acquisition by working class persons of material possessions which puts them on an equal economic level with at least the lower strata of the middle class.
(b) The acquisition by working class persons of values, attitudes and beliefs which are characteristic of a hypothesized middle class culture, this being called the *normative* aspect of social class.
(c) The mixing together of working class and middle class persons on terms of social equality in both formal and informal social situations. This is called the *relational* aspect of social class.

[1] Goldthorpe and Lockwood, Affluence and the British class structure, *Sociological Review*, **11** (July 1963), 133.

In setting up their typology of embourgeoisement, Goldthorpe and Lockwood assume that economic equality already exists and concentrate on the other two elements to suggest *one* way in which the process could occur.

Regarding the normative aspect of social class, two possibilities are suggested for the working class person:

(a) His values, attitudes and beliefs are primarily working class, i.e. his *reference group is working class.*

(b) His values, etc., are primarily middle class, i.e. his reference group is middle class.

Regarding the relational aspect of social class, two further possibilities are suggested:

(c) That the working class person is socially integrated into a membership group whose values, attitudes and beliefs he shares, i.e. his *membership group* is the same as his reference group.

(d) That he is socially isolated from membership groups whose values, etc., he shares, i.e. his membership group is different from his reference group or else he has no membership group.

The logical combination of these possibilities forms the following typology.

|  | (a)<br>Working class values | (b)<br>Middle class values |
|---|---|---|
| (d) Isolated from<br>reference group | (B)<br>Privatized worker | (C)<br>Socially aspiring worker |
| (c) Integrated with<br>reference group | (A)<br>Traditional worker | (D)<br>Assimilated worker |

The process of embourgeoisement would then be in stages. From (A) to (B) would be a process of withdrawal or separation from social interaction with other working class persons. From (B) to (C) would be a process of identification with the middle class way of life combined with a desire to be accepted as a social equal. Stage (C) to (D) occurs when the aspirant has been accepted by middle class persons and there is full social interaction.

By breaking the process down in this way one can generate testable propositions and avoid facile generalizations about the disappearance of the working class, based upon voting figures, the purchase of washing machines and the size of the family income.

The clarification of concepts is closely linked with the task of specifying propositions and hypotheses. It is desirable that propositions be stated in as formal a way as possible so that (a) logical errors may be more readily detected and (b) so that the research requirements for testing them can be specified. The most formal statement of a set of propositions takes the form of a deductive system consisting of symbolic expressions which can be manipulated by mathematical rules, i.e. by the use of a calculus. This degree of formalization is rare in sociology and existing examples would be out of place in an introductory textbook. It is possible, however, to attain a lesser degree of formality by careful reasoning allied to conceptual clarification. Certain fundamental questions may be asked: What assumptions are implied in these propositions? Do they display logical consistency? If they are true, what observable consequences will follow?

The article by Goldthorpe and Lockwood, already quoted, provides a good example of the specification of assumptions. The proposition that working class persons are being assimilated into the middle class implies several prior propositions which need confirmation:

1. That there are adequate motivations for working class persons to reject the values and attitudes of their own class.
2. That they are exposed to and accept middle class values.
3. That there are opportunities for them to mix with middle class persons in social situations.
4. That there is full acceptance of working class persons into the middle class.

Apart from revealing implicit assumptions in this way, the general process of specification also involves breaking down propositions or ideas into lower-level hypotheses which are testable by observation. The trouble with many of the propositions put forward in the name of sociology is that they are not testable. The result is that proponents can illustrate their plausibility at great length while critics can illustrate their implausibility in equal length. As long as the propositions lack empirical reference points, however, no decision can be made. They are, in fact, beyond the realm of science. An illustration of this can be found in studies defending or attacking the proposition that the structure of power in local communities is a social class structure, i.e. that in every community there is an upper social class which rules in its own interests and is in conflict with the lower classes. A recent review of such studies by Nelson Polsby makes it clear that the social class explanation of community power has been widely illustrated, but has never been brought down to the level of testable hypotheses.[1] Polsby sets himself the task of doing this, and his analysis opens the way to progress in this area of study.

## THE TESTING OF HYPOTHESES

Assuming that we have clarified our concepts and specified our propositions in testable form, the crucial task remains of designing research to actually verify the propositions. Before going into the logic of research design, it will be helpful to describe in general terms the stages of the verification process.

The first stage requires the investigator to anticipate all possible outcomes of the observations to be made, and decide which of these will be taken as refutations of a hypothesis and which will not. The decision must be made *prior* to the observations, otherwise contrary results may be "explained away" or the requirement of proof may be shifted in order to preserve a cherished hypothesis.

[1] Nelson W. Polsby, *Community Power and Political Theory*, Yale University Press, 1963.

The next stage is to determine what results actually occur. This is essentially the problem of measuring the properties of phenomena. It is necessary to distinguish between three *levels of measurement*. These will be described briefly in increasing order of precision.

The simplest and most basic form of measurement in any science is classification, i.e. the *nominal* level of measurement. This refers to the allocation of units of analysis to categories, so that the units within each category are homogeneous on selected characteristics. An example would be the classification of voters according to party reference. The categories are not ranked at this level, but they must include all cases under observation, and not allow one case to be in more than one category; that is to say, the categories must be *exhaustive* and *exclusive*.

Where categories or individual units can be ranked in terms of "greater" and "lesser" or "higher" and "lower", but it is impossible to say *how much* greater or higher, then we have what is called the *ordinal* level of measurement. A familiar example in sociology is the ranking of persons according to occupational prestige; this being used frequently as a social class ranking.

At a still higher level of precision, we have *interval* measurement, involving the quantification of distance between units. This implies the use of a stable *unit* of measurement such as an inch, a second or an ounce, as well as a reliable *instrument* of measurement such as a ruler, clock or set of scales. Intelligence tests are sometimes thought of as approximations of interval scales, but if person "A" has an I.Q. (Intelligence Quotient) of 90, person "B" an I.Q. of 100 and person "C" an I.Q. of 110, we cannot state with confidence that "B" is exactly halfway between the other two in intelligence. The question of whether intelligence tests can be called true interval scales is still problematical; this also applies to the various personality tests and attitude scales which have been developed.

## THE LOGICAL DESIGN OF RESEARCH

We turn now to the problem of designing proof that a hypothesized relationship in fact exists. The basic designs of such proof from a logical point of view were set out in the nineteenth century by John Stuart Mill. These "methods of experimental inquiry", as he termed them in his *System of Logic*, specify the requirements for inferring a causal relationship between two variables. They do not, in themselves, establish the *direction* of causality, this requires additional information about the variables, e.g. their ordering in time, which Mill does not concern himself with in the logical designs.[1]

Two of the designs are basic to experimentation, long thought of as *the* scientific method. These are the *Method of Agreement* and the *Method of Difference*. The former states that if an observation (A) is made in two or more situations which have *only one* circumstance, (B) in common, then (A) and (B) are causally related. The negative statement of the method of agreement is that where the absence of (A) is accompanied by the absence of (B) in situations having nothing else in common, then (A) and (B) are causally related. Due to the practical difficulty of finding or creating situations of this kind Mill saw these as being useful in identifying significant causal factors and suggesting hypotheses rather than in establishing proof.

For Mill the most perfect of the designs was the *Method of Difference*. This states if an observation (A) is made in one situation where (B) is present, but is not made in another situation, identical *except for* the absence of (B), then (A) and (B) are causally related. This is the logical basis for what can be called the "classical" experiment. It involves the observation of two groups, as near as possible identical. Into one of these, the *experimental group*, is introduced a factor hypothesized to have certain effects. The other group, called the *control group*, is left alone, as required by the method of difference.

Samuel Stouffer,[2] the American social scientist, has expressed the "classical" design in diagrammatic form. This is helpful

[1] For a discussion of some solutions to the problem of causal priority in social research, see Herbert Hyman, *Survey Design and Analysis*, Free Press, 1955.

[2] S. Stouffer, Some observations on study design, *American Journal of Sociology*, 55 (1950), 355.

not only in understanding the design itself but also deviations from it.

### *"Classical" Experimental Design*

Before After

| | Before | After | | |
|---|---|---|---|---|
| Experimental group | $X$ | $X_1$ | $d = X_1 - X$ | If $d$ is larger than $d'$ then the |
| Control group | $X'$ | $X'_1$ | $d' = X'_1 - X'$ | hypothesis is supported. |

The original choice of significant factors depends on the investigator and even the most perfect experimental design cannot guard against the possibility that one of these has been omitted or left uncontrolled. This is one reason why theory is so important in science, it helps in making decisions on factors of possible significance.

An important part of the design is the matching of the two groups. There are three main ways of performing this operation. For convenience we shall assume that individuals are the units of analysis, this being most commonly the case in social research.

1. *Precision matching*, where for each individual in the experimental group there is a corresponding individual in the control group, as near as possible identical in selected characteristics. This is the most accurate method of matching but in practice is often difficult to apply because each additional matching factor drastically reduces the number of people who can be paired.

2. *Matching by frequency distributions*, sometimes called quota matching. In this method the groups are matched on overall or average characteristics, e.g. by having the same average age, the same proportion of males and females, etc.

3. *Randomization*. This method is associated particularly with R. A. Fisher, the British statistician.[1] It involves the random

[1] See R. A. Fisher, *The Design of Experiments*, University of Edinburgh, 1949.

allocation of individuals to either the experimental or the control group. The procedure allows for the possibility that relevant factors have been overlooked by ensuring that the influence of such factors will be equally divided between the groups.

The "classical" experimental design has been widely used in social psychology, particularly in studies of attitude change, communication, leadership, social learning and the functioning of small groups.[1] It has found only a limited application in sociology as a whole, for a variety of reasons. The following are among the more important:

1. The sociologist is concerned with complex phenomena which are not easily subjected to controlled experimentation. Also he is interested in processes of change which may take years or even centuries to be completed.

2. Theories capable of generating precise hypotheses and specifying relevant variables are only just being developed in sociology. This makes for difficulty both in designing research and integrating results.

3. There are ethical as well as practical difficulties in using human beings for experimental purposes. The physical scientist can deliberately destroy matter or infect animals with a disease, but similar activities on the part of the social scientist such as stimulating juvenile delinquency or racial prejudice would be seen as either criminal or immoral.

While these difficulties inhibit the application of the experimental method in its "classical" form, they do not prevent it entirely. Also it is possible to apply the *logic* of experimental inquiry even though the actual design of research may deviate

---

[1] See, for example, D. Cartwright and A. Zander, *Group Dynamics*, Evanston, Row, Peterson, 1953; C. Hovland, A. Cumsdaine and F. Sheffield, *Experiments in Mass Communication*, Princeton University, 1949; A. Bavelas, Communication in task-oriented groups, in D. Lerner and H. Lasswell, eds., *The Policy Sciences*, Stanford University, 1951. There are references to experiments on these and other topics in textbooks on social psychology, e.g. P. Secord and C. Backman, *Social Psychology*, McGraw-Hill, 1964.

from the "classical" model. Apart from deviations of *design* there are also deviations of *procedure*. We shall briefly describe and illustrate these two kinds of deviation.

## PROCEDURAL DEVIATIONS

1. Instead of the experiment being undertaken under specially created, controlled conditions, as in the laboratory, it may be undertaken in "real-life" or "field" conditions.

2. Instead of the experimenter actively introducing experimental stimuli himself, he may passively observe the effects of stimuli introduced by other agencies, e.g. political, administrative or commercial agencies. An example is provided by Charles Y. Glock[1] in a review of the applications of the panel technique to the study of change. The technique involves the recruitment of a sample of individuals who are then interviewed at two or more points in time. In one study reported by Glock a sample of 503 white Christians living in Baltimore was recruited and interviewed prior to the local showing of a film called "Gentleman's Agreement", which was expected to reduce feelings of anti-Semitism. The sample was divided into those showing high, medium and low degrees of this attitude. After the film had been shown the same sample was again interviewed to assess changes in anti-Semitism. Some attempt to meet the requirements of a control group was made by comparing those who had seen the film with those who had not. A slight reduction in anti-Semitism was found among the former but not the latter, indicating that the film (the experimental stimulus) had a limited effect. The experiment was passive in that the investigators took advantage of an event introduced by another agency rather than introducing it themselves.

"Field" studies are often passive in this sense, but not invariably so. Festinger, Schachter and Back,[2] for example, in a well-known

---

[1] Glock, Some applications of the panel method to the study of change, in P. Lazarsfeld and M. Rosenberg, eds., *The Language of Social Research*, Free Press, 1955.

[2] L. Festinger, S. Schachter, and K. Back, *Social Pressures in Informal Groups*, chap. 7, New York, Harper, 1950.

study of two housing estates for married students at the Massachusetts Institute of Technology, deliberately introduced information regarding the tenants' organization into two selected groups in order to study processes of informal communication. In effect there were two experimental groups, rather than one experimental and one control group, so that there was a deviation of design rather than of procedure from the "classical" experiment.

3. Instead of being present at the introduction of an experimental stimulus, the investigator may only be able to make observations after the event. The procedure then is to trace back the causes of present effects, or else to measure the present effects of a known past situation. Ernest Greenwood[1] has called this retrospective type of experiment the "*ex post facto* experiment". Procedurally it deviates from the more familiar "projective" design in that the matching of groups is done after the event through the manipulation of records concerning individuals. An example is Helen Christiansen's[2] study of the relationship between school progress and subsequent economic adjustment undertaken in the 1930's. From an original list of 2127 pupils who had left four schools in St. Paul in 1926, Christiansen drew an experimental group of individuals who had graduated from high school and a control group of pupils who had dropped out of school early. The two groups were matched *individually* on sex and nationality but this reduced the numbers so much that other variables such as age, father's occupation and mental ability were matched by frequency distributions. Finally, two groups of 145 each were left for comparison on economic adjustment; measured by occupational advancement in terms of salary changes. The results were in line with the hypothesis that school progress is positively related to economic adjustment, but were hardly conclusive. One of the disadvantages of controlling a large number of variables and allowing only one to vary is that the effect of cumulative

[1] E. Greenwood, *Experimental Sociology*, New York, King's Crown Press, 1945.
[2] See F. Stuart Chapin, *Experimental Designs in Sociological Research*, New York, Harper, 1947.

interaction between variables is controlled and the experimental effect may only be slight.

## DEVIATIONS OF DESIGN

Stouffer's diagram of the "classical" experimental design shows four boxes representing four sets of observations. Deviations from the design occur through the inability of the investigator to fill all four boxes. There are three major types found in social research:

1. Where only an experimental group is observed before and after an experimental stimulus, this is sometimes called a "successional experiment". Diagrammatically it appears as follows:

|  | Before | After |
|---|---|---|
| Experimental Group | $X$ | $X_1$ |

The absence of a control group makes it difficult to assess what would have happened in the absence of the stimulus, and whether, in fact, a causal relationship exists. Observed changes might be due to other factors than the experimental factor. A famous example of successional experimentation is contained in the Hawthorne Study, carried out by Mayo, Roethlisberger, Dickson and others, at the Hawthorne Works of the Western Electric Company in Chicago.[1] The initial phase of the study included an experiment on how different levels of lighting affected productivity. The average output of three shops under normal conditions was established, and the level of lighting in all three was progressively raised. As expected, the level of output also rose. When, however, the lighting was restored to its previous level, output remained at the same high level. Without a control group the investigators could not be sure that there was in fact any relationship between lighting and output. Subsequent experiments, using control groups, led

[1] F. J. Roethlisberger and W. J. Dickson, *Management and the Worker*, Harvard University Press, 1939.

them to conclude that the significant factors were psychological, e.g. the mere consciousness of being special objects of study. From this point the focus of the research shifted to social psychological processes and many important generalizations about interaction in small groups were established.

2. Another variant from the "classical" design is where one group is observed before the experimental stimulus and a second group, matched with the first, is observed afterwards. In diagrammatic form this appears as:

Before     After

$X$

$X'_1$

The *assumption* is that both groups were similar before the stimulus and that differences between the two show the existence of an experimental effect. It is always possible, however, that an observed difference was initially present and not due to the experimental factor. The design is most often used in cases where the "before" group cannot be kept under observation. Examples can be found in studies by Samuel Stouffer and his colleagues[1] on the training of American soldiers during the Second World War. It was difficult to keep track of the soldiers once they had left training camp in America, so that the investigators had to find other groups for subsequent comparisons.

3. When the investigator makes observations of two groups after the effects have occurred, the design appears as follows:

After

$X_1$

$X'_1$

[1] In S. Stouffer *et al.*, *The American Soldier*, Princeton University, 1949.

*The American Soldier* also contains examples of this variation of the "classical" design. Stouffer and his colleagues tested the idea that more favourable attitudes by white soldiers towards Negro soldiers could be induced by putting entire platoons of Negroes into white infantry companies. It was hypothesized that this would occur through personal interaction and fighting side by side against a common enemy. After several months these experimental companies were compared to control companies where Negro soldiers had not been introduced. In the former 7 per cent of white soldiers disliked the idea very much compared to 62 per cent in the control group. In order to make a valid inference of a causal relationship, however, it would have to be shown that the two groups were *initially* similar in their attitudes towards Negroes. This was partly achieved by asking the soldiers in the experimental group to remember how they had felt when the idea was first announced; 67 per cent said they had initially opposed it. In effect retrospective questions were used to try and fill in the other boxes, giving the following design:

|  | Before | After |
|---|---|---|
| Experimental group | $X$ | $X_1$ |
| Control group | $X'$ | $X'_1$ |

## ESTABLISHING ASSOCIATIONS BETWEEN VARIABLES

The "classical" experimental design is based upon the occurrence or non-occurrence of factors, i.e. they are treated as attributes in a *qualitative* form. In practice, however, the observation of factors is often *quantitative* in form, i.e. we measure *degrees* of the occurrence of *variables*, rather than observe the occurrence or non-occurrence of *attributes*. The methodological problem then is to relate changes in the quantity of one variable to changes in the quantity of another. Further elaborations of this problem lead, in one direction, to discussions of statistical techniques such as correlation analysis. We shall not follow this direction, however, because of the complexity of the subject matter. We can move in another, less technical, direction by considering the logical basis of this kind of analysis. Once again John Stuart Mill provides a useful starting point. One of his methods of inquiry, the *Method of Concomitant Variations*, states that if variations in the amount of one variable are associated in a *regular* way with variations in the amount of another, then there is a causal relationship between them. If an increase in one is associated with an increase in the other, then we refer to a *positive association*. If the increase in one is associated with a decrease in the other, then we refer to a *negative association*. The method can be applied in conjunction with an experimental design but it has been utilized in sociology primarily as a substitute. The same problems of proof arise here as in "classical" experimentation, i.e. the possible influence of unknown or uncontrolled factors, the *significance* of comparisons between groups, and establishing the *direction* of causality.[1]

One of the most famous examples of the application of the method of concomitant variations in sociology is Emile Durkheim's study of suicide rates.[2] In establishing an association between religious affiliation and suicide rates, Durkheim begins by presenting tables showing that predominantly Protestant European countries had suicide rates about three times as high as predominantly Catholic countries. He then asks whether the differences would be attributed to broader social and cultural differences rather than specifically to religion. In order to explore this possibility Durkheim then compares Protestant and Catholic provinces within the state of Bavaria, these provinces being similar in other respects. The procedure is repeated for Prussia, and in both cases the differences in suicide rates persisted. Durkheim was then able to conclude that there was a genuine causal relationship between

---

[1] For a discussion of this problem, see Hubert M. Blalock, *Causal Inferences in Non-experimental Designs*, University of North Carolina, 1964.
[2] Durkheim, *op. cit.*

the two factors and went on to explore the nature of the relationship.

Durkheim's study serves to illustrate the point that once a *statistical* association between two variables has been established, the investigator must check that this in fact reflects a real *causal* relationship. The appearance of a relationship can be given if two variables are both independently determined by a common third variable. If we call the two statistically associated variables the *independent* variable (this being the hypothesized determining factor) and the *dependent* variable (this being the hypothesized effect), and call the common third factor the antecedent variable, then a false or *spurious* relationship can be represented as follows:

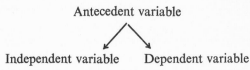

Antecedent variable

Independent variable    Dependent variable

The lines indicate that the antecedent variable is *causally prior* to both other variables and will produce a statistical association between them even though no causal relationship exists. Where such a demonstration of spuriousness is made we can refer to the *explanation* of a relationship.[1]

An example of the search for spuriousness is provided in a recent article by Harry J. Crockett.[2] The general proposition examined by him is that a strong achievement motive[3] leads to more realistic striving, greater effort, greater persistence and, therefore, to greater achievement than a weak motive. After using data from several existing studies to demonstrate a statistical association between achievement motive and the occupational mobility of sons relative to their father's occupation, Crockett asks whether the association

[1] For a discussion of this and other ways of elaborating a statistical association between two variables, see Hyman, *op. cit.*

[2] Crockett, The achievement motive and differential mobility, *American Sociological Review.* **27** (Apr. 1962), p. 191.

[3] See David McClelland *et al.*, *The Achievement Motive*, New York, Appleton–Century–Crofts, 1953.

might be explained away by antecedent variables which determine both factors. He selects five likely variables: occupational prestige of father, age level, amount of formal education, marital status, and the presence of children in the home. The empirical problem is to compare two groups who are high and low on achievement motive but similar on these five variables, in terms of occupational mobility. In order to make the comparison, Crockett uses the method of precision-matching. Due to the rapid attrition of cases he was unable to match on all five variables simultaneously, but matched on three at a time, repeating age level. In both matchings the association between achievement motive and occupational mobility persisted, so that there is evidence of a genuine causal relationship. An interesting finding, however, was that the relationship only held for those whose fathers were in lower prestige occupations, not for those whose fathers were in higher prestige occupations. Crockett suggests that the achievement motive is more significant in determining the mobility of lower class males than upper-middle class males, i.e. that the variable operates differently according to social class background. This is an example of another type of elaboration of a statistical association, called the *specification* of a relationship. This is our next topic.

Often a relationship is demonstrably genuine, but needs to be specified in terms of the conditions under which it is maximized or minimized. This is particularly useful in reconciling previously contradictory findings. Miller and Hamblin[1] in a review of 24 studies concerning the relative effect of co-operation and competition on the productivity of small, task-orientated groups, point out that in 14 of these competition was more effective while in the others co-operation was more effective. The authors examine the possibility that by specifying the situations under which the results were obtained, these findings might be reconciled. They classify the situations according to whether the tasks performed involved a high or a low degree of interdependence between members of the groups, i.e. whether group output was a co-operative

[1] L. Miller and R. Hamblin, Interdependence, differential rewarding and productivity, *American Sociological Review*, **28** (Oct. 1963), p. 768.

product of the sum of individual products. They then propose the following hypotheses:

1. Under conditions of *high* task interdependence the amount of group productivity will be *inversely* related to the differential rewarding of individual members, i.e. to competition.
2. Under conditions of *low* task interdependence group productivity will be *directly* related to competition.

Miller and Hamblin use data of their own to support these hypotheses, thereby specifying the original relationship.

Finally we shall describe a third way of elaborating a relationship, this being referred to as *interpretation*. As in the case of explanation a third variable is introduced, but instead of being causally prior to both the others it is seen as an *intervening* variable, determined by one and determining the other. It may be represented as follows:

Independent variable → Intervening variable → Dependent variable

As in explanation the original statistical association is greatly reduced by the introduction of a third variable, but here the variable is an essential part of the relationship and helps in understanding it, rather than demonstrating spuriousness. An article by Lewis Lipsitz[1] provides an example.

Authoritarianism has been defined as a set of interrelated personality traits which includes a rigid adherence to conventional values, a submissive attitude towards idealized authority figures, an aggressive attitude towards "out-groups" and a predisposition to accept anti-democratic solutions to political problems. Seymour Lipset[2] has argued that the lower class way of life is particularly conducive to "rigid and intolerant approaches to politics".[3] He refers particularly to a low level of education, low participation in

[1] Lipsitz, Working class authoritarianism, *American Sociological Review*, **30** (Feb. 1965), p. 103.
[2] S. Lipset, *Political Man*, New York, Doubleday, 1960.
[3] *Ibid.*, p. 101.

voluntary associates, economic insecurity, and authoritarian family patterns as explanatory variables. Lipsitz examines the hypothesis that education is the main intervening variable in interpreting the relationship between social class and authoritarianism. Statistically this means that if the level of education is controlled then lower class people will be no more authoritarian than middle class people. Data is presented from three national opinion surveys undertaken in the United States, showing a clear association between social class and authoritarianism. When comparisons are made between working and middle class respondents *with equivalent levels of education*, however, the differences disappear. Lipsitz's conclusion is that lower class people are more authoritarian because they receive less education.

## THE COMPARATIVE METHOD

As we have seen, both experimentation and the establishment of concomitant variations involve making comparisons. In some textbooks, however, reference is made to "the comparative method" as an approach distinguishable from both of these.[1] The examples usually given to the method appear to include two kinds of investigation.

The first kind involves the use of data from two or more societies or two or more cultures, but the design used is some form of experimentation or statistical analysis. The word comparative, in this case, refers to *sources* of the data or to the *context* of the research, not to the method of analysis. We have already referred to Durkheim's study of suicide rates; this is a good example of cross-cultural research. A more recent example is Seymour Lipset's work on the economic conditions favourable to democratic political institutions.[2] Several European and Latin-American countries were classified as being "more democratic" or "less democratic", then within the two areas comparisons were made on

[1] For example, T. Bottomore, *Sociology*, pp. 48–51, London, Allen & Unwin, 1962; and M. Duverger, *Introduction to the Social Sciences*, pp. 261-267. Allen & Unwin, 1964.

[2] Lipset, *op. cit.*, chap. II.

indices of economic development. Lipset concluded that democratic institutions are more likely to appear and survive the higher the level of economic development. As in Durkheim's study, the basis of the research design was the method of concomitant variations. It is clearer to refer to this kind of cross-cultural study as *comparative analysis* rather than as an application of *the* comparative method. This kind of analysis is not *methodologically* distinct from other research, but as Robert Marsh has made clear in a recent article,[1] it does have a special role to play in the development of sociology as a science. The main contributions described by Marsh are:

1. Cross-societal analysis broadens the range of variables to be explained[2] and therefore tests the explanatory power of a theory.
2. The replication of studies done in one society in other societies of a *similar type* helps establish generalizations.
3. Replication in societies of a *different type* carries the process of generalization even further.
4. Where attempts at replication fail, there is a challenge to existing theory, this may lead, for example, to conceytual clarification or the specification of a relationship.

The second type of study often quoted under the heading of "the comparative method", also uses cross-cultural data, but deals with complex phenomena in widely differing societies or over long periods of time and makes no claim to testing limited hypotheses. The concern is with exploring a general thesis or with making stimulating contrasts and comparisons. Statistics may be used to supplement descriptions or to support particular points but no attempt is made to quantify variables in order to establish precise causal relationships. An outstanding example of

[1] Robert M. Marsh, The bearing of comparative analysis on sociological theory, *Social Forces*, **41** (Dec. 1964), p. 188.
[2] Marsh cites the work of George Murdock based on the Human Relations Area Files at Yale University, e.g. Murdock, Anthropology as a comparative science, *Behavioral Science*, **2** (1957), 249.

this kind of research is provided by Max Weber's comparative studies of religion.[1] The starting point of these studies was a concern to understand certain unique features of Western European civilization such as the progressive rationalization of life, which in the economic sphere is manifested as capitalism. In some early essays, published in 1904–5 as *The Protestant Ethic and the Spirit of Capitalism*, Weber sought to show that there were "psychological affinities" between the characteristic attitudes and values of Puritanism and those characteristic of capitalism. He did not claim a direct causal link but argued that the psychological and behavioural implications of Puritanism contributed significantly to the creation of a social-cultural environment favourable to the development of capitalism. Weber subsequently undertook a comparative study of the civilizations of China, India and Ancient Palestine to show how the ethics of various religious doctrines had either encouraged or inhibited economic development (i.e. in historical terms capitalism). Weber is concerned with the significance of religious doctrines partly at the level of psychological consequences and individual behaviour, especially economic behaviour, and partly at the level of social organization, particularly the distribution of prestige and power. The latter approach leads him to examine particular status groups, such as the literati in China and the Brahmins in India, so that the analysis shades into political sociology at many points. Weber develops empirical generalizations which can be made into testable hypotheses[2] but the focus of inquiry is the understanding of certain unique features of Western civilization and why they did not appear or develop fully elsewhere. In other words, he is concerned with the interpretation of historical phenomena rather than the building up of general theory. This kind of broad comparative study is, in fact, better referred to as *historical sociology* because this indicates both the kind of data used and the focus of inquiry.

[1] Max Weber, *The Sociology of Religion*, Boston, Beacon Press, 1963. For an excellent summary of Weber's comparative studies in this and other areas of sociology, see R. Bendix, *Max Weber: An Intellectual Portrait*, Heineman, 1960.

[2] Bendix, *op. cit.*, pp. 277–278.

## SOURCES OF DATA AND METHODS OF
## SOCIAL INVESTIGATION

Having discussed the design of research we conclude the chapter with a review of the major sources of information available to the sociologist and some methods commonly used to exploit them. Because of the scope of the subject and the scarcity of space we limit ourselves to brief dictionary-type definitions and leave the reader to pursue particular topics elsewhere.[1]

A preliminary point to be made is that a major source of information is the work of other social scientists. This is implied in the notion of a *cumulative* creation of knowledge, basic to any science. The utilization of this source to formulate or test hypotheses is often referred to as *secondary analysis*. The articles by Lipsitz and Crockett, cited above, are examples. In this section, however, we are concerned only with original or primary sources. These may be divided into two major categories: documentary data and human beings. We shall discuss methods of investigation under these two headings.

### DOCUMENTARY DATA

*A. Qualitative documents.* Under this sub-heading we include sources such as newspapers, books, diaries, biographies, films and radio programmes. These can be analysed in either a quantitative or a non-quantitative way. A classical study utilizing documents in a non-quantitative way is Thomas and Znaniecki's work on Polish migrants to America.[2] The study was concerned with conditions in Poland encouraging migration to America in the early twentieth century and with the integration of migrants into American society. The largest single source of information was a collection of several hundred letters, written by migrants, and acquired through an advertisement in a Polish–American journal.

[1] Two useful introductory textbooks are M. Duverger, *op. cit.*, and W. Goode and P. Hatt, *Methods in Social Research*, McGraw-Hill, 1952.

[2] W. I. Thomas and F. Znaniecki, *The Polish Peasant in Europe and America*, 1st ed., Boston, Gorham Press, 1918–20.

The second largest source consisted of the archives of a Polish newspaper, purchased by Thomas during a visit to that country. A third source was made up of letters written by prospective migrants to the Emigrants Protective Society. Znaniecki was director of this organization in Poland from 1911 to 1914. The method used to exploit this massive collection of documents was essentially that of the historian or literary critic, i.e. careful interpretation based upon knowledge and experience.

The *quantitative* analysis of qualitative documents is most commonly undertaken through a method called *Content Analysis*. Bernard Berelson, a prominent exponent of the method, has defined it in terms of four basic characteristics.[1]

1. It is typically limited to the *manifest* content of documents, particularly of communications, and only indirectly to latent intentions or effects.
2. Categories of analysis are developed to classify the content of particular documents; these must be defined precisely enough to yield the same results if applied by different analysts. In this sense the classification is objective rather than being a matter of personal interpretation by an investigator.
3. The categories must be related systematically to research problems or to hypotheses. The whole content must be classified in order to avoid a biased selection of evidence.
4. The results must be expressed quantitatively either through stating numerical frequencies for each category or by using quantitative terms such as "more", "always", "often".

Berelson discusses seventeen different topics to which the method has been applied; these range from analyses of trends and changes in the content of mass media communications to studies of the givers and receivers of communication. Reference should be made to Berelson's article for further readings.

Although content analysis is the most widely used method for

[1] Berelson, Content analysis, in G. Lindzey, ed., *Handbook of Social Psychology*, vol. 1, chap. 13, Addison–Wesley, 1954.

the quantitative study of documents, attempts have been made to develop other methods. An example is the attempt to apply mathematical graph theory to the analysis of narrative accounts of individual behaviour.[1]

*B. Quantitative documents.* Under this sub-heading we include official statistics and records. A particularly important source of this kind is census data, collected by governments for administrative and informational purposes. Around this source has developed the special discipline of demography, concerned with the size and structure of populations. Demography has developed its own statistical techniques for analysing this kind of information.[2] In sociology quantitative data may be used directly in establishing empirical generalizations, as in Durkheim's study of suicide rates which was based upon official records. Alternatively it may be used indirectly to construct indices of abstract concepts. This refers back to the problem of operational definitions raised previously. An example is Lipset's study of economic development and democracy.[3] He used sources such as United Nations statistical reports to construct indices of economic development, e.g. wealth was indicated by *per capita* income and thousands of persons per motor car, industrialization by percentage of males in agricultural occupations and urbanization by the percentage of people in cities of 100,000 or more.

### HUMAN BEINGS AS SOURCES OF INFORMATION

We shall discuss six methods of utilizing this basic source of data.

1. *The sample survey.*[4] This is the most important single method of investigation used by the sociologist. It is particularly important in collecting original statistical information and in establishing relationships between variables by the method of concomitant

[1] See Charles Dailey, Graph theory in the analysis of personal documents, *Human Relations*, **12** (1959), 65.

[2] For example, Margaret Hagood, Selected techniques for population data, in *Statistics for Sociologists*, New York, Holt, 1941.

[3] Lipset, *op. cit.*

[4] See Herbert Hyman, *op. cit.*

variations. The sample survey attempts to make generalizations about a specified population by studying a representative sample. Preferably the sample should be drawn according to well-established principles of probability theory so that its representativeness can be measured. Practical difficulties sometimes make for deviations from these principles, however, and consequently there may be difficulty in deciding how far given results can be generalized or what population can be generalized to. This is particularly the case where the "sample" consists of a convenient group of people, e.g. university students or residents in a single locality. In such cases there is no sample in the statistical sense of the word.

Another important characteristic of the method is the use of a *standardized questionnaire*. This means that questions are pre-tested to eliminate ambiguity, and other obstacles to accurate information, also that the same questions are asked in the same way of all respondents.[1] One of the main advantages of standardization is that it is easier to quantify the responses and to make use of mechanical counting procedures, e.g. through punch-card machines or computers.

2. *Intensive interviewing*. This is most usefully employed in exploratory studies or in conjunction with standardized questionnaires. It is distinguished by the extent to which the respondent is encouraged to talk freely and in depth about particular topics. Insights may be obtained about experiences, attitudes and motivations which are useful in generating hypotheses or in interpreting statistical relationships.[2]

3. *Participant observation*. This is a method developed primarily by anthropologists in studying simple or primitive societies, which has been incorporated into sociology. Like intensive interviewing this method utilizes to the full the social skills of the investigator. A well-known work based upon participant observation by a single investigator is William F. Whyte's study of

---

[1] The construction of a questionnaire is a specialized task, too complex to be discussed here; see Goode and Hatt, *op. cit.*, chap. II.

[2] For a discussion of a "semi-structured" method of interviewing see R. K. Merton, M. Fiske and P. Kendell, *The Focussed Interview*, Free Press, 1956.

"Cornerville", a slum area of Boston.[1] He was introduced into the local community through an influential resident, referred to as "Doc", who was the unofficial leader of the Norton Street Gang; one of several gangs on the periphery of the local "underworld". Whyte undertook a long period of participation and observation based upon his friendship with Doc, concentrating particularly on personal interaction in the context of informal groups and on the relationships between such groups in the context of local politics and crime. Apart from its substantive findings the book is interesting for methodological comments on participant observation generally.

An example of participant observation by a team of investigators is the Lynds' study of a Mid-Western community during the 1930's.[2] Members of the team lived in private households and joined fully in the life of the community, attending "churches, school assemblies and classes, court sessions, political rallies, labour meetings, civic club luncheons, missionary meetings, lectures, annual dinners, card parties, etc."[3] These observations were supplemented by documentary data, informal interviews and standardized questionnaires to produce a detailed analysis of the community.

4. *Controlled observation*. The essence of this method is the use of *trained* observers who record on-going behaviour in terms of *pre-defined* categories. It has been used mainly in studying face-to-face interaction in small groups, e.g. families, committees, discussion groups and work groups. The observer does not participate directly so that the method is particularly suitable where the presence of a stranger might distort or disturb interaction. It also overcomes the difficulties involved in asking people to report on their own behaviour or on the significance of their behaviour from the point of view of group functioning.

An outstanding example of research utilizing this method is the

[1] W. F. Whyte, *Street Corner Society*, University of Chicago, 1943.

[2] Robert S. Lynd and Helen M. Lynd, *Middletown*, New York, Harcourt, Brace, 1937.

[3] *Ibid.*, Appendix on Methodology.

work of Robert F. Bales and his colleagues at Harvard University.[1] Apart from the actual findings of the research it has stimulated many other studies[2] and constitutes an important step forward in the study of human behaviour. The assumption underlying Bales's work is that small groups reveal regular patterns and types of interaction, which occur in some form regardless of the personalities of members and of specific group aims. In order to reveal such patterns there must be a continuous classification of small units of interaction in terms of standardized categories. Bales developed his categories through looking at existing classification systems, observing a variety of groups, and developing theoretical propositions. At one time he had as many as 85 categories, but the final system consists of only 12. We cannot discuss these in full but they include categories like "shows solidarity", "gives opinion", "shows tension release", "agrees", "gives suggestion". These are all related systematically to theoretically defined dimensions of group interaction and problem-solving processes. The theoretical development of Bales's system has been linked to the structural-functional model of social systems as elaborated by Talcott Parsons.[3] We shall refer to this in a later chapter.

On the methodological side, Bales himself has spent much time in developing technical equipment, such as one-way mirrors and recording systems, and in developing training procedures for observers.

5. *Sociometric measurement.*[4] This method is also concerned with personal interaction. It is basically a means of analysing and representing the structure of attractions, rejections and lines of communication existing in a group at a given time. In its simplest form, the method involves asking the members of a group which

[1] R. F. Bales, *Interaction Process Analysis*, Cambridge, Mass., 1950.

[2] For a review of subsequent developments see Bales, Small group theory and research, in R. K. Merton, L. Broom and L. Cottrell, eds., *Sociology Today*, New York, Basic Books, 1959.

[3] See T. Parsons, R. Bales and E. Shils, *Working Papers in the Theory of Action*, Free Press, 1953.

[4] Sociometry is particularly associated with J. L. Moreno, *Who Shall Survive?* (1934). See also Helen H. Jennings, *Sociometry in Group Relations*, Washington, D.C., American Council on Education, 1948.

other members they would choose or not choose in connection with specified activities. The choices can, if desired, be presented in diagrammatic form with circles to represent members and lines to represent choices or rejections. This is called a *sociogram*. Sociometric techniques, some of them based on sophisticated mathematical formulae, have been widely used in studying leadership, morale, prejudice, popularity and social adjustment. Mostly in laboratory or "natural" small groups but also in local communities. Examples of these and other applications can be found in a journal called *Sociometry*.

6. *Attitude scales*. The attitude scale consists typically of a set of standardized statements, chosen to reflect an underlying personality trait such as conservatism, authoritarianism or racial prejudice. In what is called a Thurstone scale, after the psychologist L. L. Thurstone, judges are used to sort a large number of statements into piles. Thurstone himself used eleven piles. These are arranged progressively from the lowest to the highest reflection of the underlying attitude. A scale value can be given to each statement according to its allocation in the series of piles by several independent judges. A selection is then made of the best statements to represent the full range of scale values. This being done on the basis of statistical formulae. The statements are presented to the respondent who is asked to check the statements with which he agrees. His total score is then the average of the scale values of the statements he chooses.

Another major form of the attitude scale is named after Rensis Likert. In the preliminary stage of constructing a Likert scale, items are chosen by the investigator on the basis of experience, knowledge and theoretical definition. The respondent is asked to indicate how far he agrees or disagrees with each one. Typically there are five possible choices, "strongly agree", "agree", "uncertain", "disagree", "strongly disagree". Arbitrary numerical values are given to each choice, e.g. 1 for "strongly agree", 2 for "agree", and so on. The scores of an individual on the items are averaged to give a single attitude score. It is common practice to choose a large number of items to begin with and then use methods such as interval consistency or the discriminative power of each item, to make a final selection of items for the standardized scale.[1] In all attitude scaling the two main problems are to ensure *reliability*, i.e. that a scale will consistently produce the same results when applied to the same sample, and to establish *validity*, i.e. that the items really refer to the underlying attitude it is wished to measure.

Louis Guttman has also raised the problem of unidimensionality, i.e. ensuring that a scale measures only one attitudinal dimension rather than reflecting two or more.[2] This is related to attempts to develop attitude scales of sufficient precision to qualify as interval scales. At the present time, however, they remain superior forms of ordinal measurement.

[1] For a discussion of these points see Goode and Hatt, *op. cit.*, chaps. 15 and 17. Also M. Jahoda, M. Deutsch and S. Cook, *Research Methods in Social Relations*, Part I, chap. 4, New York, Dryden, 1951.

[2] See Guttman's description of scalogram analysis in S. Stouffer *et al.*, *op. cit.*, vol. 4, *Measurement and Prediction*.

# CHAPTER 2

# SOME SOCIOLOGICAL DEFINITIONS

THE main purpose of this chapter is to introduce the student to some of the basic concepts which appear in the theoretical and empirical writings of sociologists. We have already referred to the difficulties which are involved in taking familiar terms and then trying to refine them into scientific concepts. These difficulties are most apparent in the research situation where the looseness permissible or even useful theoretical speculation becomes a handicap. There is a discernible progression from "common-sense" thinking about social phenomena to attempts at scientific verification which involves an increasing need for rigour and precision in the use of words. When the same term is used throughout this progression, as happens in newly developed sciences such as sociology, then some ambiguity is inevitable. In the speculative stage of outlining problems and generating ideas, the value of a term is judged by its usefulness in ordering thoughts or in stimulating the imagination. At this stage thinking is essentially exploratory and some looseness in definition is needed to avoid rigidity and sterility. In the research stage, however, the requirements of measurement and verification demand very precise definition. Most of the terms considered in this chapter reflect the attempts of sociologists to proceed from one stage to the other. They are not presented as precise technical terms as would be the case for a textbook in a mature science, but as verbal reference points which will help the student to grasp the sociological approach to social phenomena as well as preparing him for future excursions into the literature. Most of the terms are familiar in everyday language and there are no esoteric formulae to be learned.

We said in the first chapter that the sociologist is concerned with regularities in social life. As applied to individuals involved in social behaviour the search for regularities can move in three directions. In the first place one can study social behaviour in terms of *cultural* regularities such as rules of behaviour, customs, values or beliefs. Cultural elements exist as objective facts embodied in written or spoken language which impinge upon the individual as restraints or guides to behaviour; they also exist as personality factors which have been *internalized* through social learning processes. Thus there is an overlap with a second direction for sociological inquiry, viz. the interpretation of social behaviour in terms of underlying personality factors such as attitudes, opinions, needs and goals. A third direction is to concentrate on the way specific social acts cohere as patterns in collectivities of individuals. Regular patterns of behaviour performed by individuals as members of collectivities are called *roles* which are limited to specific *positions*. When we have two or more role-positions forming a persistent unit of interaction then we may refer to a *social system*. When the concern is with the positions, i.e. the static aspect of a social system, then we refer to a *social structure*. Quite often the social structure of a particular collectivity is presented diagrammatically as a set of boxes or circles connected by lines showing the kind of relationship which exists within the set of positions. The clearest examples occur in studies of formal organizations where positions are officially defined for administrative purposes.

The smallest type of social system consists of two actors and is called a *dyad*. Real life units such as the family, the club, the neighbourhood and so on may be analysed as social systems, though varying in size, type of interaction and activities engaged in. The largest and most comprehensive type of social system studied by sociologists is called a *society*.

We have organized our discussion of concepts in terms of the three directions which the search for social regularities may take: (a) cultural elements; (b) the individual as social actor; (c) units of social interaction.

## CULTURAL ELEMENTS

Culture was developed as a social scientific concept by anthropologists in the nineteenth century. Their primary concern was to distinguish social heredity, i.e. the passing down of culture from one generation to another, from biological heredity; to distinguish men from other animals. They used culture in an all-embracing way to include every aspect of social behaviour which could be thought of as distinctively human. According to Edward Tylor, the English anthropologist, culture is "that complex whole which includes knowledge, belief, art, morals, law, custom and any other capabilities and habits acquired by man as a member of society".[1] A more recent definition by the American anthropologist, Kroeber, echoes this omnibus definition of culture as "that which the human species has and other social species lack . . . speech, knowledge, beliefs, customs, arts and technologies, ideas and rules . . . what we learn from other men, from our elders and the past, plus what we may add to it".[2] The development of social science during the 1950's and 1960's has seen persistent efforts to narrow the concept for analytical purposes. One of the outstanding efforts was made by Kroeber and Talcott Parsons.[3] They restricted the concept to refer to the "transmitted and created patterns of values, ideas and other symbolic-meaningful systems as factors in the shaping of human behaviour".[4] This emphasis on the ideal and the symbolic distinguishes culture from actual behaviour. In fact the degree to which behaviour approximates to cultural "blueprints" is a central problem in sociology. Where these blueprints are *moral* rules then lack of correspondence between them and behaviour is manifested as immorality or perversion. If these rules are also embodied in the legal system then deviance from them is manifested as delinquency or crime. Where the blueprints are *cognitive* in character, e.g. mathematical rules, engineering techniques or rules of

[1] E. Tylor, *Primitive Culture*, p. 2, London, John Murray, 1891.

[2] A. Kroeber, *Anthropology*, p. 253, New York, Harcourt, Brace, 1948.

[3] A. Kroeber and T. Parsons, The concepts of culture and social system, *American Sociological Review*, **23** (Oct. 1958).

[4] *Ibid.*, p. 583.

experimental procedure, then deviance is manifested as stupidity, inefficiency and so on. In the case of *aesthetic* blueprints, deviance is manifested as bad taste or ugliness. In each case cultural standards are used to evaluate behaviour or the products of behaviour. The products include such diverse phenomena as machines, buildings, poems, symphonies, scientific theories, the limited company and the examination system in British universities. These are created by human agents acting in a cultural context, but we do not include them in the definition of culture unless the products themselves are ideals, values or beliefs. In other books the student may find references to the "material" culture, indicating the kind of product which can be seen, touched or heard.

The student may be concerned about the gap between the sociological definitions of culture indicated above and the more familiar humanist definition which emphasizes the activities and products of artists and intellectuals. Such a concern has been felt by some sociologists for many years and a recent article by two American sociologists attempts a reconciliation between the "humanist" and "scientific" concepts of culture.[1] The origin of culture, so the argument runs, lies in the encounter of human beings possessing universal needs and psychological mechanisms, with the limiting conditions of the environment. The culture-creating act springs from a confrontation of the person with an impersonal setting; it is an effort to invest the social and physical environment with personal relevance and meaning. To be human is to be a seeker or creator of self-relevant meaning. The products and major resources for continuing the quest for meaning are *symbols*. In order to clarify the meaning of a symbol the authors define it as a special type of *sign*. There are three different processes in the use of signs:

1. *Indication*, where an object or event serves as an indicator of something else, e.g. where sneezing is perceived as an indicator of a cold. Signs of this kind are interpreted as having a *causal* link with the referent.

[1] G. Jaeger and P. Selznick, A normative theory of culture, *American Sociological Review*, **29** (Oct. 1964), 653.

2. *Denotation*, where the sign stands for something else in a specific but non-causal way. It may be an object as when a red light stands for danger, but usually it is a word, e.g. the word "table" stands for a whole class of objects with specific characteristics.

3. *Connotation*, where a word not only has a denotive meaning but evokes other associations and meanings also. The word "house" denotes a class of objects, but for a given person it may also connote security or warmth. A connotive sign like any other must show a certain stability of association between itself and the referent so that purely personal and arbitrary associations are excluded from the discussion. A symbol may be defined as a sign which is responded to *directly* as a vehicle of connotative meaning. It is in itself a focus of meaningful experience, capable of arousing feelings and ideas in a fairly stable, predictable way amongst people sharing the same culture. The symbol is a perceptible embodiment of emotionally meaningful experiences and is used to re-evoke or reinforce the feelings associated with the original experience. Any repetitive act or human artefact can become a symbol but to be a *cultural* symbol it must be public, i.e. available to all actors in a social system as a vehicle of meaning.

The definition of culture arrived at by Jaeger and Selznick is that it "consists of everything that is produced by and is capable of sustaining shared symbolic experience".[1] The products of human activity must therefore possess symbolic significance in a social system before they are included as part of a culture.

The connection between this sociological definition of culture and humanist definitions of "high" culture is that both involve the use and creation of symbols. The main difference is that in "high" culture the process tends towards self-concious expertise and symbols become the product of skilled effort rather than the outgrowth of shared experiences in society.

The most significant implication of this particular definition of culture is that it attempts to introduce the possibility of evaluation into the prevalent neutral approach to cultural phenomena.

[1] G. Jaeger and P. Selznick, *op. cit.*, p. 663.

The aim is to go beyond description and analysis so that the investigator can judge one culture or part of a culture as better than another. The criterion of judgement is that some symbols do more than others to make life meaningful for the people who share them as cultural elements. A critique of a culture would be based upon an examination of the richness and comprehensiveness of symbolic experience in everyday life. The measurement of these imprecise qualities is not discussed by Jaeger and Selznick, but some indicators are suggested which might help in this task. We have presented this particular definition of culture as a stimulating challenge to accepted sociological theory and one or two words of criticism are called for. The theory appears to be unduly narrow in its insistence that nothing is cultural unless it can be shown to function as a vehicle of "expressive symbolism". We referred previously to moral rules which exist as guides to social interaction and to cognitive rules which act as guides to intellectual activity. Many of these would be excluded from the notion of culture by Jaeger and Selznick because they are technical or utilitarian in character and do not carry expressive meanings to any significant extent. It may be useful to distinguish symbolic from other cultural elements as constituting a particular area of culture with its own distinctive characteristics, but it appears arbitrary and unnecessary to call this the whole of culture.

So far we have referred to culture as a universal phenomenon created out of human interaction without distinguishing between culture in general and *a* culture as a particular cluster of "blueprints" in a given social system. A social system may be anything from a two person family to a whole society including great numbers of smaller social systems. Therefore within a society there will exist a multitude of cultures. In so far as the observer is concerned with interpreting these as variations of the societal culture, then they may be referred to as *sub-cultures*. This term occurs frequently in studies of deviant or poorly integrated groupings such as juvenile delinquents or racial minorities. When the concern is with a particular social system in its own right, however, the sociologist often refers to the culture of a factory or a gang or a neighbourhood without relating it to a broader cultural context in a systematic way.

## Values and Norms

These are two of the most frequently used terms in defining elements of culture and some examination of them is necessary. Harold Fallding, in a recent analysis of the concept *value*, defines it as "a generalized end that guides behaviour toward uniformity in a variety of situations, with the object of repeating a particular, self-sufficient satisfaction".[1] Familar examples of values are wealth, loyalty, independence and friendliness. These generalized ends are consciously pursued by or held up to individuals as being worthwhile in themselves. Fallding's definition is heavily biased towards a psychological conception of values and refers primarily to individual motivation. For this reason he becomes involved in the problem of distinguishing a value from other motivating factors such as pleasures, interests and compulsions. The basic drawback of the psychological approach is that it focuses attention on individual behaviour and away from cultural elements which exist independently of particular individuals. The strategy of research is shifted towards inferring of values from individual actions and verbalizations of motive; this detracts from the study of values as cultural elements embodied in language. It also obscures the crucial problem of how cultural elements, including values, are transmitted to individuals. Weaknesses in cultural transmission produce discrepancies between public values and individual motivations which challenge the social order. To confuse these two things by a psychological definition of values is to confuse the analysis of this problem. As a preliminary definition of a value we might describe it as a verbal symbol for a generalized end which has connotations of rightness, goodness or inherent desirability. Values not only enter into personal behaviour as

[1] H. Fallding, The empirical study of values, *American Sociological Review*, 30 (Apr. 1965), 224.

motivating or restraining factors, but also into social system interaction as means of legitimizing authority, mobilizing support or reinforcing morale. The generalized ends may refer not only to the condition of the individual, but also to that of a group. This is particularly apparent in political speeches during times of real or contrived crises. Regardless of the reference point, however, values exist as cultural elements in a historical context and can be studied as such independently of the observation of individual behaviour.

There is rather more agreement concerning the definition of a *norm* than that of a value. It is a statement of expectation, requirement or demand concerning the behaviour of a social actor. A norm differs from a value in that it is more specifically directive in content; it tends to be instrumental or utilitarian rather than expressive or symbolic. Norms can be classified in many ways but the most important distinction is between those in which the *proscriptive* element is strongest and those in which the *prescriptive* element is strongest. A *proscriptive norm* is one which directs a role-player to avoid or abstain from a certain type of activity. A *prescriptive norm* is positive in form and spells out forms of behaviour which role-players are expected to follow, e.g. the goals they are expected to achieve and the means by which they are to pursue them.

The former tend to be more inflexible in that behaviour is defined as *either* compliant *or* deviant, whereas prescriptive norms involve behavioural *degrees* of conformity.[1]

All norms are maintained by *positive* and *negative* sanctions (i.e. rewards and punishments), but vary greatly in the strength of the sanctions involved. For example, the punishment for eating peas with your fingers at a dinner-party may be no more than a raised eyebrow and some degree of ostracism; whereas the punishment for violating a more serious norm such as a taboo or law may be death or imprisonment.

[1] For elaborations of these and other qualities of norms, see E. Mizruchi and R. Perruci, Norm qualities and deviant behavior, *American Sociological Review*, 27 (June 1962), 391.

Related to differences in the strength of sanctions are differences in the way these are administered and the agents who do the administering. The main distinction here is between *formally* designated administration, e.g. by lawcourts, and *informal* administration, e.g. by friends or colleagues. The greatest degree of formalization occurs in the *institutionalized* areas of social interaction. This term will be discussed more fully in a later chapter but we may note at this point that all large-scale social systems are faced with recurring problems which must be solved if the system is to maintain itself as a going concern. At the simplest level there are problems of feeding, clothing, the organization of work, the maintenance of order and the induction of children into the cultural system. The role-positions and activities which develop as solutions to these problems are grouped into fairly well-defined clusters, e.g. economic, political, legal, religious and familial. Institutionalization refers to the organization of normatively directed behaviour around problems of significance for the maintenance, survival or successful adaptation of a social system. The more usual term for this kind of role cluster is a *social institution*.

Reference has been made to sanctions as a means of ensuring conformity to norms and we may call this the *collective control* of behaviour. A more efficient way of achieving this aim is for individuals to internalize such controls through training, education and example. The process by which norms and other behavioural regulators are transformed into personality elements is called *socialization*. Conscience is one characteristic product of this process. Socialization of a basic kind is undertaken within the context of the family but the process occurs throughout the life-cycle as an individual undertakes new roles in various social systems. Defects in the socialization process may arise in various ways: through personality dispositions or mental incapacity, through interruptions to social learning, through incoherence or contradiction in the social environment. Like many of the significant topics in sociology, the socialization process overlaps with psychological concerns—in this case with learning and the formation of personality.

## THE INDIVIDUAL AS SOCIAL ACTOR

For many contemporary sociologists the basic unit of social behaviour and the logical building-block for sociological theory is the *social act*, i.e. the interplay between the action of the self and the expected or actual reaction of one or more others. One of the outstanding figures in the development of this kind of analysis was Max Weber, working in the tradition of nineteenth-century German students of social action. In the area of general sociology, Weber's main concern was to construct a typology of social action for use in the analysis of historical data. In observing human behaviour, the sociologist is faced with the problem of interpreting the meaning of what others are doing. Weber suggests two approaches to the interpretation of meaning: (a) by identification with an actor so that the observer attempts to re-live the meaning of an action as it was experienced by an actual participant; (b) by constructing types of action from experience or knowledge and interpreting behaviour as approximations to these constructs. This is the basis of Weber's method of "pure" or "ideal" types; the purity is an intellectual or logical one and contains no evaluative implications.

In setting up his classification of action, Weber chose *rational action* as the most convenient and readily definable pure type, and treated emotional or other non-rational behaviour as deviations from this conceptual yardstick. Weber's classification is as follows:

1. *Zweckrationalitat* or "pure" rationality, in which the actor employs rationally appropriate means to attain rationally selected ends.
2. *Wertrationalitat*, in which the means are rationally appropriate but the ends themselves are non-rational, e.g. culturally determined or emotionally determined.
3. *Traditional* or habitual action, e.g. action which follows a ritual pattern or takes the form of etiquette.
4. *Affective* or emotional action.

In analysing a particular event such as a political campaign in an election, Weber would first of all determine what the course of action would have been if the actors were purely rational and then introduce other factors such as custom or emotion to explain observed deviations from this hypothetical construct.[1]

The most elaborate attempts to develop social action analysis in contemporary sociology are found in the works of Talcott Parsons.[2] He does not follow the "ideal type" approach of Weber but deals with the same problem of classifying behaviour on the basis of the motivations and aims of the actor. One of Parsons's early classifications runs as follows:[3]

1. *Cognitive motivation* (i.e. a desire for accuracy or truth), which is manifested in action as an *intellectual orientation* to objects or people. Objects are perceived in terms of general standards applied as universal yardsticks regardless of personal feelings or particular relationships with an object.

2. *Cathectic motivation* (i.e. positive-negative reactions of an emotional kind), which is manifested in action as an *expressive orientation* to objects. In this case personal feelings are given primacy over "objective", rational considerations.

3. *Evaluative motivation*, which may either be *moral* in direction and manifested as a *responsible orientation* or concerned with means towards given ends (e.g. in evaluating two alternative solutions to a problem) in which case there is an *instrumental orientation*.

Given sufficient verbal ingenuity there are many classifications of action that could and indeed have been devised. The above examples, however, are good illustrations of the terminology of action theory and have also been incorporated into empirical research. In both cases the classification was a preparation for the

[1] Max Weber (trans. A. Henderson and T. Parsons), *The Theory of Social and Economic Organization*, Free Press, 1947.

[2] See, for example, T. Parsons, *The Structure of Social Action*, New York, McGraw-Hill, 1937.

[3] For elaborations of this and other classifications see T. Parsons and E. Shils, *Toward a General Theory of Action*, Harvard University Press, 1951.

analysis of social organization so that they are of some importance in sociological theory.

A very important and widely used concept in studying individual behaviour is that of *attitude*. The concept has been intensively developed by social psychologists and focuses attention on the personality rather than upon the social act; upon predispositions to act in a certain way rather than upon the classification of action.

In general terms an attitude may be defined as a predisposition to evaluate objects or other aspects of the social environment in a favourable or an unfavourable way.[1] Daniel Katz, an American social psychologist, has attempted to specify the dimensions of an attitude for measurement purposes, basing his discussion on a distinction between the affective (emotional) and cognitive components of attitudes. Among the dimensions he specifies are the following:

1. *Intensity*, which refers to the strength of the emotional component.
2. *Specificity-Generality*, which refers to the cognitive clarity of an attitude, i e. the extent to which it has been given definite intellectual shape by an individual holding it.
3. *Degree of differentiation*, which refers to the sheer number of cognitive elements in an attitude, regardless of their clarity.
4. *Centrality*, which refers to the relevance of an attitude to values important for the individual, i.e. the extent to which the attitude is embedded in his personality system or bound up with his self-concept.

Katz goes on to analyse attitudes in terms of the functions they fulfil for the individual, this being necessary in order to specify the conditions under which they may change. Given the function of maximizing rewards and minimizing punishments (i.e. an *instrumental* function), then change may be effected by changing

[1] For a review and analysis of the concept see F. De Fleur and M. Westie, Attitude as a scientific concept, *Social Forces*, **42** (Oct. 1963), 17.

an existing pattern of rewards and punishments or by encouraging different aspirations. Such an attitude is held for expediency or the sake of social adjustment and is relatively easy to change. Another possible function of an attitude is *to protect the ego* from perceived threats and change may be effected by encouraging self-insight as in psychiatric treatment. A third function is to provide a ready means of understanding or interpreting events in the environment, i.e. a *cognitive* function. In this case change may be induced by giving more meaningful information about these events or by rational persuasion. Campaigns designed to change attitudes must be guided by an awareness of their functional significance for the people who hold them in order to be effective.

As a conclusion to this section we will draw attention to what has been called the "dramaturgical" approach to social interaction. This recent development in sociology is concerned with analysing behaviour as it occurs in the physical presence of others. The outstanding figure in the dramaturgical approach is Erving Goffman, and the following remarks are based on his work.[1]

When a person appears before others in a social context his words, gestures and actions will convey impressions of him; the individual therefore attempts to control the presentation of himself so as to convey desired and convincing impressions. In order to analyse the process of impression management, Goffman resorts to theatrical terminology. He sees the social actor as giving performances before various audiences and using strategies either to project an image or to maintain the continuity of a performance. The "props" for his performance include not only personal attributes such as dress, speech or manner, but also physical settings such as furniture, lighting or status symbols. When interaction is disrupted, then confusion or embarrassment ensues and various mechanisms are called into play to restore continuity, e.g. a humorous reference to the cause of the disruption. Goffman also goes into the question of collective impression management and "team performances" as in the case of doctors and nurses

[1] See E. Goffman, *The Presentation of the Self in Everyday Life*, University of Edinburgh, 1956.

when hiding the brutal facts of death or disease from hospital patients.[1]

## UNITS OF SOCIAL INTERACTION

As we indicated in the introduction to this chapter, units of social interaction are seen as clusters of role-positions which form social systems. Unfortunately there are real-life social units, e.g. London, Britain, Europe, which can be meaningfully referred to as administrative, geographical, political or economic units but which lack the degree of coherence implied in the term social system. Nonetheless, it has been found useful to analyse complex social units of this kind as though they were systems of inter-dependent elements and we shall concentrate on theoretical definitions rather than on the description of specific, real-life units.

### Society

Following Edward Shils[2] we may describe a society as a self-reproducing social system within whose territorial and cultural boundaries the life of most of its members is lived. From the individual's point of view it is the most enduring, comprehensive and extensive of the various social systems he may belong to. For the sociologist the qualities of persistence and cohesion shown by societies constitute a major area of inquiry; the term *macro-sociology* is used to describe this area of study. Shils suggests that the problem of cohesion is best approached by studying personal attachment or identification with institutions, objects and persons who symbolize the wider society. More specifically there exist major sub-systems such as the economy, the polity, religious institutions, the educational system and so on which contain

[1] For a broad interpretation of the significance of Goffman's work see B. Glaser and A. Strauss, Awareness contexts and social interaction, *American Sociological Review*, 29 (Oct. 1964), 669.

[2] E. Shils, in D. Ray, ed., *Trends in Social Science*, pp. 60–83, New York, Philosophical Library, 1961.

organizations having decision-making elites. Their decisions are made in accordance with certain standards and values, some of which are observed by all authoritative role-players. These standards and values comprise the *central value system* of the society; the centrality is both moral and authoritative. It is this central value system which provides the focus for cohesion, order and identity in a society.

At a less comprehensive level than the whole society there exists a large body of empirical research focused upon the *community*. In many cases the term refers to a particular town or village in a "common-sense" way. There have been many attempts to refine the concept, however, and these have taken two distinct directions. The first direction is illustrated by the work of Ferdinand Tönnies[1] in the nineteenth century. He defined a community as an organic, "natural" kind of social collectivity whose members are bound together by a sense of belonging, created out of everyday contacts covering the whole range of human activities. Tönnies contrasted this type of collectivity with another, called an *association*, which is consciously organized for specific purposes and whose members are bound together by common regulations or interests. In contemporary sociology the organic conception of community appears as a kind of ideal to be pursued by town planners or as a style of life which is in danger of being destroyed by the impersonal, fragmented contacts associated with large-scale urban areas in industrialized societies.

The second direction taken in refining the concept of community is related to the development of *human ecology* as a separate branch of the social sciences. In its contemporary form human ecology focuses upon the physical structure of society as determined by the way economic resources are allocated.[2] One of its major concerns is with patterns of land usage as determined by economic profitability. The basic unit of observation is the community conceived as the area of daily interaction for an aggregate

[1] See F. Tönnies (trans. C. Loomis), *Community and Association*, Michigan State Press, 1957.

[2] See A. Hawley, *Human Ecology*, New York, Ronald Press, 1950.

of persons. A fuller definition of community, arising out of ecological studies, is a collectivity the members of which share a
common territorial base of operations for daily activities. No
reference is made to belongingness, close personal contacts or
other elements central to the kind of definition presented
previously.

An attempt at even greater refinement, based upon the ecological approach, has been made by Talcott Parsons.[1] Instead of
treating community as a particular kind of social unit, Parsons
defines it as one aspect of all social units. More specifically, it is
that aspect of a social system referrable to the territorial location
of human beings and their activities. Residence, which is related
to income and social class, constitutes one element in defining
community structure. Another element is jurisdiction which
imposes rules and authoritative decisions on people living within
spatially defined areas. Parsons discusses other elements but the
main point is that the fact of territorial location is reflected in such
phenomena as social class residential areas, distinctive industrial
or business areas, territorial administration and transportation
systems. The study of the community aspect of social systems
would concentrate on this kind of phenomena and on the role-
positions associated with them.

We said previously that the term community is used in an
omnibus way to refer to a wide variety of specific social units.
George Hillery[2] has attempted to distinguish two qualitatively
different types from the various empirical units which are lumped
together as communities. On the one hand there are folk villages
and cities, which Hillery classifies as "vills"; on the other hand
there are closed communities such as hospitals, prisons and mental
homes, which he classifies as "total institutions" (following
Erving Goffman's usage).[3] The *vill* is described as a *localized*
social system integrated around *families* and *co-operation* for

[1] T. Parsons, *Structure and Process in Modern Societies*, Free Press, 1961.
[2] G. Hillery, Villages, cities and total institutions, *American Sociological Review*, **28** (Oct. 1963), 779.
[3] See E. Goffman, *Asylums*, New York, Doubleday, 1961.

limited purposes. In the city co-operation is based upon contracts and membership of formal associations as well as upon family-based personal co-operation. Localization refers to territorial identity and spatial location.

A *total institution* is characterized by a staff of "officials" which compels a localized population of inmates to behave in a closely regulated way. Between the staff and the inmates there exists a basic antagonism that permeates the whole social system. Hillery goes on to construct detailed descriptive models of these types and uses empirical data to show that the differences are qualitative and not merely a matter of degree. One of his conclusions is that the distinction between community and non-community collectivities may be best conceptualized as a difference between those designed to attain specific goals and those which have at best only diffuse goals. This follows very closely the distinction between community and association elaborated by Tönnies but goes further in specifying the characteristics of communities and in drawing a conceptual distinction between these and other social units.

## The Group

Here again we find a variety of social phenomena gathered under one omnibus heading. The term group has been used to describe anything from a football crowd to a whole society. In social psychology it refers to an aggregate of persons small enough in numbers to interact at a face-to-face level. There is, moreover, an assumption that interaction persists over a reasonable period of time, at least long enough for some definite structure of positions and roles to emerge. George Homans has written a stimulating book on this type of group which has become a minor classic in sociology.[1] Apart from the empirical generalizations and conceptual clarifications contained in the book, it is interesting as an attempt to establish the small group as the basic unit of social theory and observation rather than the social act.

[1] G. Homans, *The Human Group*, London, Routledge & Kegan Paul, 1951.

The term *primary group* was originally coined by Charles Cooley, a pioneer American sociologist, to refer to groups characterized by intimate face-to-face association. They are primary chiefly in the sense of forming attitudes, opinions and values, i.e. as agents of the socialization process. There is considerable overlap with the concept of community as defined by Tönnies but it also includes play groups, informal work groups and the family.

Empirical research on primary groups has been concerned with such problems as the conditions under which solidarity develops amongst members, the emergence of leaders as a function of group problem-solving, the formation of cliques within groups, the effective incorporation of new members and the processes by which the group adjusts to its environment. Apart from the impressive volume of studies undertaken under controlled laboratory conditions,[1] the main emphasis has been on the functioning of informal small groups within the context of formal organizations, such as industrial, administrative and military bureaucracies. An outstanding example of this kind of research is the series of investigations carried out in the Hawthorne works of the Western Electric Company.[2] The investigators began in an orthodox way by studying the effects of lighting, hours of work, length of breaks and so on, upon output, but gradually turned their attention to the significance of informal groups for morale and efficiency. They found, for example, that work groups developed their own norms regarding output which were in conflict with the output targets defined by management. The effects of incentive schemes or bonuses could not be predicted unless the intervening influence of informal groups was taken into account.

The importance of the primary group has also been demonstrated in studies of voting and public opinion.[3] In the formation of public opinion on current issues, much attention has been paid

[1] For an attempt to integrate the findings of laboratory studies, see J. Thibaut and H. Kelley, *The Social Psychology of Groups*, John Wiley, 1959.

[2] See F. Roethlisberger and W. Dickson, *op. cit.*, Harvard University Press, 1939.

[3] See, for example, P. Lazarsfeld, B. Berelson and H. Gaudet, *The People's Choice*, Free Press, 1944.

to the "two-step flow of communication".[1] Instead of conceiving of messages flowing *directly* from newspapers, radio, television and other mass media to an audience of individuals, public opinion analysts see them as flowing to a selective, attentive audience of informal leaders of opinion who transmit the messages to others through primary group interaction. Obviously a great deal can be lost or added in translation.

Studies such as those indicated above show the continued vitality and importance of primary groups even in large-scale society. They provide a salutary antidote to theories of mass society which posit an increase of anonymity, impersonality and alienation in society as a consequence of the supposed destruction of primary group ties. We shall return to the notion of "mass society" in a later chapter.

In conclusion we would remind the student that it is fruitless to seek the "right" or "true" meaning of a scientific concept, although it is legitimate to ask what the true meaning of a word is for social actors in a given context. We have attempted to discuss some sociological terms as scientific concepts and have indicated the vagueness and ambiguity which surrounds even commonplace terms. In general the student should adhere to definitions which have proved useful in guiding or interpreting research but must avoid the temptation to use words in an omnibus way to cover qualitatively different phenomena.

[1] For example, E. Katz, The two-way flow of communication, *Public Opinion Quarterly*, **21** (Spring 1957); also E. Katz and P. Lazarsfeld, *Personal Influence*, Free Press, 1955.

# CHAPTER 3

# THE SUBJECT MATTER OF
# SOCIOLOGY

OUR discussions of sociological methods and concepts have given some indication of the kind of topics dealt with by sociologists but we must now attempt a more specific delineation of their subject matter. This is in fact a difficult task because sociology is only one of several disciplines concerned with human activity. The growth of specialized disciplines may be explained in various ways but the following factors are particularly important:

(a) In the academic sphere, as in the industrial, efficiency is increased by the division of labour and the cultivation of limited expertise;

(b) Expertise itself is a more saleable and "rewarding" commodity than general knowledge. Professional careers are built upon specialized training rather than on breadth of scholarship;

(c) Specialized disciplines tend to become self-perpetuating through being embodied in the organizational-administrative systems of educational bodies. Obviously it is in the interests of those who have identified themselves with a particular subject to maintain that subject as an academic reality, i.e. as a department or administrative unit with its own financial resources, its own promotional system and so on. The vehemence with which academics defend their subjects from the encroachments of other specialists is partly explained by this factor of professional self-interest.

Further discussion of the subject matter will be divided into two sections: firstly, what the "founding fathers" said it was or should be; secondly, what sociologists actually do.[1]

## COMMENTS OF THE FOUNDING FATHERS

*August Comte* (1798–1857)

Like Saint-Simon, with whom he associated as secretary and co-author, Comte saw the sciences as forming a hierarchy linked to the progressive development of human knowledge and the ultimate triumph of reason. At the summit of the hierarchy, there was to be a science of society called "political science" or "social physics" based upon historical observation and directed by the notion of inevitable human progress in controlling the social-physical environment. Society is seen as an entity having a reality apart from the individual; it is also more important than the individual because it is the historical embodiment of culture or civilization. The preservation of society demands not only a secular, political authority but also a spiritual authority. In the new, scientifically-based society envisioned by Comte the exercise of secular authority would be left to "leaders of industry" while spiritual authority would be vested in the "wisest" practitioners of social physics. They would be the priests of a new "religion of humanity" based upon a new morality of unselfish love and unquestioning obedience to authority.

Before the task of building the new society could begin, however, the "laws" governing the development of society had to be formulated. It is interesting to note that while Comte advocated "scientific" observation, on the model of physics or chemistry, he rejected the application of statistics in social science. So adamant was Comte on this point that he coined the word *sociology* to replace "social physics" because the latter had been used by the Belgian statistician Quetelet as the title of a book.

In his programme of study Comte distinguished between *social*

[1] The general outline of the discussion is taken from A. Inkeles, *What Is Sociology?*, New York, Prentice-Hall, 1964.

*statics* and *social dynamics.* The former is concerned with the anatomy of society, with the effects and counter-effects which the component parts have on each other. The latter, and for Comte the more important section, was in effect a documentation of a general "theory" of the natural progress of mankind towards scientific rationality. This progress follows the so-called law of the three stages of intellectual development; the first stage was that of theological thought, dominated by priests, then followed the metaphysical stage which led into the stage of scientific positivism at the end of the eighteenth century.

The basic unit of society for Comte was not the individual but the family, where the individual as a social being is created. Although there is much that is pretentious and discredited in Comte's work, it is possible to discern certain continuities between his thinking and the following elements of contemporary sociology:

1. The concern with scientific observation as opposed to metaphysical explanation or moral evaluation. In Comte's work itself there is a systematic illustration of preconceived historical patterns rather than any testing of hypotheses. Nonetheless the aspiration was a vital change of approach at the time he was writing.
2. The idea of society as a system of interdependent parts which has both a structural and a functional aspect.
3. The conception of the sociologist as an active participant in social affairs or as an agent of change.[1] Apart from participation in governmental, industrial or other agencies and the conduct of policy-oriented research this conception may refer to the sociologist as someone who indulges in debunking, usually at the cost of established authority, in unrespectability, by studying topics beyond the pale of middle-class propriety, and in cosmopolitanism, by advocating tolerance, openness and variety in human relations.[2]

[1] For a contemporary view of this position see C. Wright Mills, *The Sociological Imagination*, New York, Oxford University Press, 1959.

[2] These terms are taken from Peter L. Berger, *Invitation to Sociology: A Humanistic Perspective*, New York, Anchor Books, Doubleday, 1963.

## Herbert Spencer (1820–1903)

Like Comte, he emphasized the continuity of human history and was concerned with relating the direction of its development to his own society. In Spencer's work, however, this is seen as an evolutionary process rather than as inevitable progress; the implicit optimism of Comtean progress is replaced by a non-evaluative delineation of evolutionary stages. The general direction of evolution, in society as in nature, is from fragmentary homogeneity to cohesive heterogeneity. Spencer's classification of societies begins with the simplest type exemplified by isolated, primitive tribes and ends with large-scale industrial society. The division of labour in productive activity is one of the main evolutionary developments described by Spencer.

In analysing society as a structural entity Spencer used the analogy of a biological organism. He did not say that society was an organism, merely that biological terms are useful as a conceptual scaffolding which could be dispensed with as sociological knowledge developed. Thus, Spencer interprets the administrative, legal processes of a social system in terms of the regulative functioning of the centralized nervous system in an organism. Industrial activities are compared to the working of the autonomic nervous system and decision-making to that of the cerebrospinal nervous system.

Although Spencer's scaffolding tended to dominate the actual building there are elements of his thought which are echoed in contemporary sociology. In particular there is the idea of society as a self-regulating system of processes, tending towards an equilibrium, which is analogous to the idea of a biological organism tending towards homeostasis. The implication is that a disturbance in one part of the system, whether externally or internally caused, will be balanced by complementary changes in another part of the system. This idea is still prominent in social theory. It suffers from the difficulty of defining the actual boundaries of a social system and the degree of interdependence which must exist before a system can be said to exist. In fact there is nothing in social systems entirely analogous to the death or malfunctioning of biological organisms so that it is difficult to evaluate changes in terms of survival or better adaptive potentiality.

Although the idea of unilinear evolution (i.e. going in one irreversible direction) has been abandoned, the continuing concern of sociologists with social change has resulted in a revival of evolutionary thinking, though in modified form.[1] The following quotation from an article by Robert Bellah illustrates the contemporary approach: "Evolution at any system level I define as a process of increasing differentiation and complexity of organization which endows the organism, social system or whatever the unit in question may be, with greater capacity to adapt to its environment."[2] Bellah dissociates himself from any implications of inevitable or irreversible change, but there is a clear continuity with the evolutionary tradition represented by Spencer.

## Emile Durkheim (1858–1917)

Durkheim is, apart from Max Weber, the most directly influential of the founding-fathers of sociology. Like Comte he was concerned with establishing propositions on a scientific basis but he criticized Comte both for *assuming* the existence of cultural evolution rather than inferring it from data or treating it as a hypothesis, and for applying the idea of evolution to an amorphous humanity rather than to specific societies. Spencer he saw as avoiding the second error but committing the first. Durkheim himself saw the historical succession of societies as branches on a tree rather than forming a single continuum.

A key concept in Durkheim's attempt to establish sociology as an empirical science was that of the *social fact*. Social facts are characterized by their potentiality for constraint or coercion relative to the individual. They are exterior to individuals and

[1] See Julian H. Steward, *Theory of Culture Change*, University of Illinois, 1955.

[2] R. Bellah, Religious evolution, *American Sociological Review*, 29 (June 1964), 358. This issue also contains other articles on evolution.

cannot be reduced to psychological data. The criterion of extern-
ality can only be understood as part of a revolt against the individ-
ualistic conception of action, accepted by utilitarianism, where it
is seen as the rational pursuit of *subjectively* determined ends.
For an empirical science of society to exist it must deal with
facts which are resistant to subjective wishes and as real in their
effects as those dealt with by the natural sciences. The clearest
examples of social facts are moral beliefs or legally sanctioned
norms. However there also exist social facts at a less obvious level,
such as trends, currents of opinion and mass movements which
impinge on the individual without his being necessarily conscious
of what is happening or of how his behaviour fits into a collective
pattern.

The reality of society for Durkheim lay in its values, ideas and
beliefs; the more intense and frequent social interaction is, the
greater the likelihood that such integrative elements will be created.
Through interaction the private sentiments of individuals are
transformed into social facts. This process is seen as a kind of
chemical synthesis which results in new entities called "collective
representations"; these are more than mere aggregates of individual elements and must be studied in terms of their own
characteristics. The principal social phenomena such as religion,
ethics, law, the economy, the polity, were seen by Durkheim as
modes of conduct, beliefs and values instituted by the collectivity.
Sociology he saw as the study of the development and functioning
of such institutions. This must be done on a comparative basis
by analysing institutions in different types of society at comparable
stages of evolution. The basis for classifying societies into types
was similar to that of Spencer; at the simplest level is the "horde",
at the next level there are aggregates of hordes called "clans", then
the typology proceeds through the tribe and the city-state until
one reaches the "doubly compounded, polysegmental" society.

As part of his reaction against the grandiose "theories" of
Comte, Durkheim insisted that sociologists should confine their
attention to clearly defined groups of social facts and formulate
specific hypotheses about them which could be tested empirically.

The outstanding example of this approach in Durkheim's work is his study of suicide. The totality of suicides in a given society, as measured by suicide rates, is treated as a social fact which can only be explained sociologically and not by individual motivations to suicide. The concern is with variations in suicide *rates* between societies as a function of social conditions; society is the unit of analysis, not the individual. From a comparative study of rates in various European societies Durkheim derived three categories of suicide:

1. *Egoistic suicide* which results from the alienation of the individual from his social environment. This type is common where cultural factors such as those embodied in Protestantism emphasize individualism and self-centred striving.

2. *Altruistic suicide* which is found in rigidly structured societies placing a group-centred code of duties above the individual, making self-sacrifice for the group a moral command. The suicidal behaviour of Japanese dive-bomber pilots in World War II would come under this heading.

3. *Anomic suicide* which occurs when a failure or dislocation of social values leads to individual disorientation and a feeling of meaninglessness in life. This may arise through temporary dislocations like war or economic crisis; through personal factors such as rapid social mobility; or through rapid changes in the social structure, such as those associated with the industrialization of underdeveloped countries, which undermine traditional authority and established values.

In all three categories the probability of a given individual being exposed to situations conducive to suicide is determined by the social structure. Whether or not a person will actually succumb to these situations in a particular case is a matter for psychological analysis. The sociologist is concerned only with the fact that a predictable number will succumb, not with the individuals who make up the number.

In spite of his empirical orientation, Durkheim was very much concerned with the problem of making value-judgements and believed that the sociologist should be able to say what ought to be or to make diagnoses of social ills. For Durkheim the *raison d'être* of science was to help men live a more satisfying life. He therefore devoted much effort to establishing criteria of health and morbidity in analysing society. Following the example of medical science Durkheim equated health with normality; the latter, however, must be established for different societies according to their type and stage of evolutionary development. The normal, average, healthy characteristics of a society are defined as those found most frequently in the *type* of society to which it belongs. Criminality as a general characteristic is normal to all societies and as such its presence is not a sign of pathology. There are, however, particular forms and rates of crime which must be established for each type of society at each stage of evolution. Deviations from these normal forms and rates would then be diagnosed as morbid indicators of underlying social factors, injurious to the maintenance of the social system.

Durkheim's emphasis on the reality of society as something separate from the reality of individuals left him open to the accusation of setting up society as a mystic entity superior to the individual. His name has been linked with totalitarian ideologies. A close reading of Durkheim's work should convince the student that such criticisms are largely invalid and that the philosophical obscurities which occur are minor compared to the stimulating clarity of his theoretical insights and the thoroughness of his empirical research.

### Max Weber (1864–1920)

Weber's work covers a vast area of historical and sociological study; it is also rather fragmentary in nature, and this adds to the difficulty of summarizing his conception of sociology. Like Durkheim he reacted against large-scale, speculative "theories" of society and insisted on isolating specific topics for investigation.[1]

[1] For a review of Weber's lesser known excursions into empirical research of the survey type, see Lazarsfeld and Oberschall, Max Weber and empirical social research, *American Sociological Review*, **30** (Apr. 1965), 185.

He went further, however, in arguing that particular conceptual schemes must be developed for each separate topic. Durkheim concentrated on developing a general theory of society relevant to all investigations. Weber's theoretical work consists of a series of elaborate typologies which are not integrated into a general theory.

We have already referred to Weber's concern with historical-comparative research (in the first chapter) and we will merely remind the student that the aim underlying this concern was an understanding of European capitalism as experienced in his own time. It was in the pursuit of a more satisfactory approach to history that he developed his general sociology. The construction of general typologies permitted the linking together of historical case studies and the formulation of general propositions.

Weber used his typology of social action, described previously, to construct a conceptual scheme which focuses upon the conditions for the successful control of individual behaviour in society. At the primary level of analysis there are personal relationships which, if they occur regularly, over long periods of time, become institutionalized as customs or norms. Personal interaction takes place within a framework of legitimate order which may be *conventional* (i.e. deviance results in disapproval) or *juridical* (i.e. deviance results in forcible restraint by a formally designated authority). At the secondary level of analysis there is the group, defined by the closed nature of the social relations constituting it and by the presence of persons who attempt to preserve the internal order of these relations. Where relations of regular obedience exist then one can observe the exercise of power, this being the probability of a group member obtaining obedience from others. In groups with established political role-positions power takes the form of legitimately exercised coercion, i.e. *authority*.

Weber's analysis of authority has stimulated a great deal of empirical research, particularly in the study of bureaucracy. The following is a brief outline of his typology of authority, based upon the way in which it is legitimated:

1. *Rational-legal* authority is derived from the fact of occupying an official position in an organized hierarchy. It is limited by formally defined rules and is vested in the position itself not in the individual who fills the position. An organization held together by this type of authority is termed a *bureaucracy*. In contemporary research a distinction has been made between the *rational* component of bureaucratic authority which derives from the possession of specialized knowledge and the *legal* component which derives from the rules of the organization. In some cases an individual may possess knowledge without office, e.g. a staff specialist in an industrial organization; in others he may have office without specialized knowledge, e.g. a general administrator in charge of a research laboratory.
2. *Traditional* authority is based upon the sanctity of "what has always been so". This type of authority is inherited, usually on the basis of kinship.
3. *Charismatic* authority is based upon personal qualities perceived as being extraordinary and of a kind to inspire devotion or awe. This type is particularly important in creative or innovative social action, this being contrasted with the routine and the ordinary in human affairs.

Weber repeatedly emphasized that none of his "pure" types could be observed in isolation; empirical studies would show mixtures of the types. His own historical research dealt, for example, with the disruptive appearance of charismatic personalities in bureaucratic organizations and the co-existence of traditional and rational-legal authority in the same social structure.

### *Georg Simmel* (1858–1918)

Simmel, a German sociologist, has inspired a limited amount of research in contemporary sociology. Much of his work is in the form of essays which are speculative and suggestive rather than empirical or rigorously theoretical.

Simmel's conceptualization of the subject matter of sociology was similar to that of Weber in that it focused upon social action. Like Weber he thought in terms of a continuum of types of interaction ranging from spontaneous, personal encounters to permanent, repeated interactions which are crystallized into institutional structures and regulated by norms. Sociology is concerned with normatively regulated behaviour. More specifically, Simmel defined two major areas of study for sociology:

1. *General sociology*, which studies institutional phenomena on a comparative basis as advocated by Durkheim. This area also includes the study of rhythms, stages and patterns of development in society, particularly processes of growth and decline.

2. *Formal sociology*, which abstracts the normative element from actual behaviour and analyses societal forms of interaction. Examples of these societal forms are competition, conflict, superordination and subordination (in most textbooks these appear as social processes rather than forms of interaction, but this is merely a matter of convention). In one of his essays Simmel deals with sociability as a form of behaviour. Men are brought together into groups or associations by specific needs and interests but in the course of interaction a feeling of "sociation" is generated which is valued in itself quite apart from utilitarian considerations. While all units of interaction are characterized by sociation or sociability, there are some which are based purely on this feeling, e.g. the club or the party. In these cases self-interest or goal-seeking is replaced by good manners or tact in regulating egotistical impulses.

Elsewhere in his work Simmel devotes considerable attention to the analysis of conflict in society. Particularly interesting are his discussions of the *positive* functions of conflict, e.g. in relieving tensions, in providing a motivation to action or in leading to a reaffirmation of group solidarity.[1]

[1] For a systematic explication of Simmel's ideas on conflict, see Lewis Coser, *The Functions of Social Conflict*, Free Press, 1956.

In all his work there is a tendency to refer back to interaction at the small group level and one can see the influence of Simmel in the contemporary study of group dynamics.[1]

## Bibliographical Note

Students wishing to refer to the actual writings of the founding fathers should consult the following selection of books:

AUGUSTE COMTE, *Positive Philosophy*, New York, Blanchard, 1855.

HERBERT SPENCER, *The Principles of Sociology* (3rd ed.), New York, Appleton & Co., 1910.

EMILE DURKHEIM (trans. J. Spaulding and G. Simpson), *Suicide*, Free Press, 1951.

Ed. and trans., KURT H. WOLFF, *Emile Durkheim: A Collection of Essays*, Ohio State University Press, 1960.

*The Elementary Forms of Religious Life*, Free Press, 1947.

*The Rules of Sociological Method*, Free Press, 1938.

MAX WEBER (trans. A. Henderson and T. Parsons), *Theory of Social and Economic Organization*, New York, Oxford University Press, 1947.

Trans. H. Gerth and C. Wright Mills, *From Max Weber: Essays in Sociology*, New York, Oxford University Press, 1946.

GEORG SIMMEL (ed. and trans., Kurt Wolff), *The Sociology of Georg Simmel*, Free Press, 1950.

## WHAT SOCIOLOGISTS DO

The discussion of what sociologists actually study is divided into two parts: (1) substantive areas of investigation, and (2) the aims of investigation.

1. An analysis by Hornell Hart[2] of twenty-four textbooks published in the United States between 1952 and 1958 revealed twelve major areas of concern: scientific method; social theory; personality in society; culture; human groups; caste and social class; race; social change; economic institutions; family and kinship; education; religion. The study of local communities would also be included if urban and rural areas had been considered together. The labelling of the areas could be criticized on

[1] See L. Festinger, A theory of social comparisons, *Human Relations*, 7 (1954).

[2] Reported in Inkeles, *op. cit.*

the grounds that several of them overlap in actual investigations, but the list gives some idea of the concentration of effort.

In describing what sociologists study in a particular period, allowance must be made for factors in the social environment which encourage convergences of effort around particular topics. Three main types of factor may be observed:

(a) The development of easily applicable research techniques in particular fields which encourage replication or refinement. In the area of personality research there was the development of the authoritarian attitude scale which claimed to "measure" a basic personality factor by presenting a person with a list of statements to which he indicated agreement or disagreement by placing marks in appropriate boxes.[1] The "paper and pencil" technique of attitude measurement has promised high returns for little intellectual outlay and encouraged many sociologists to study personality. Another example is the development of the "reputational" technique for identifying local community leaders.[2] By assembling a panel of local "experts" on community affairs and asking them to nominate the most influential people in the community, one can quite easily build up a list of agreed leaders to be used as a basis for studying the "power structure". Recently the technique has come under heavy criticism, mainly because its adherents have tended to equate *reputation* for influence with *actual* power.

(b) There are practical problems or areas of social concern which may vary from one period to another or from one society to another; the important point is that they attract funds from political, industrial or philanthropic agencies and create convergences of research effort. This factor is particularly important in Britain with its scarcity of "free-floating" research funds and its small university departments.

[1] See T. W. Adorno *et al.*, *The Authoritarian Personality*, New York, Harper, 1950.
[2] See F. Hunter, *Community Power Structure*, University of North Carolina, 1953.

Most sociological research in Britain centres around areas of concern to policy-makers, e.g. juvenile delinquency, industrial productivity, industrial training, wastage in education, race relations and town planning. The demand for useful results allied to policy-oriented traditions of thought in the profession itself has produced a great deal of research in Britain which lacks theoretical direction or interest.

(c) Sociologists have discovered various "captive" subjects in hospitals, prisons, schools and universities whose mere availability makes for a concentration of research. In some cases the particular subjects and their environment are studied; in other cases they are used as representative social beings for the testing of general propositions. The great danger is that investigators may generalize from rather particular populations in order to increase the significance of their findings.

2. The aims of research studies provide another way of indicating what sociologists do. We have drawn up the following list:

(a) The testing of hypotheses derived *logically* from theoretical propositions. This degree of scientific sophistication is rare in sociology due to the lack of rigorous theory and the scarcity of precise measuring instruments. In recent years, however, there has been an encouraging increase in attempts at this kind of study, e.g. in the examination of small groups and bureaucratic organizations.

(b) Investigating propositions derived from speculations, hunches or loosely formulated conceptual schemes. This is the most common type of theoretically oriented research in sociology.

(c) Investigating empirical generalizations taken from previous research; these are either replications of other studies or attempts to resolve contradictory findings. This type is particularly common in American sociology and in several areas of study there exist impressive accumulations of research.

(d) Exploratory studies of some particular area of social life, which aim to prepare the way for more rigorous investigation. In some cases this is done through the secondary analysis of existing work rather than by actual research in the field.[1]

(e) Policy-oriented studies designed to throw light on problems of immediate practical concern, e.g. the incidence of poverty, the reduction of racial tension or the effectiveness of a public relations campaign.

(f) Straightforward descriptive studies focused upon a limited area of social life. Many community studies are of this kind, for example the so-called "Chicago school" centred around Robert Parks provided many excellent monographs during the pre-war period.[2]

(g) Studies aimed consciously at documenting a particular ideological or evaluative point of view. These are at the periphery of sociology conceived as a science, in that the authors reject the principle of scientific detachment as far as social research is concerned. They make their ideological convictions a central part not only of the selection of problems but also of the way they formulate and investigate them. Studies based upon Marxian ideology come into this category.

## SOCIOLOGY IN RELATION TO OTHER HUMAN DISCIPLINES

The development of knowledge concerning the social environment has been accompanied by an increasing tendency towards fragmentation into specialized disciplines and sub-disciplines. Sociology itself was one product of this process. As a reaction

[1] An excellent example is G. Homans, *op. cit.*, London, Routledge & Kegan Paul, 1951.

[2] See F. M. Thrasher, *The Gang*, University of Chicago, 1937; H. Zorbaugh, *The Gold Coast and the Slum*, Chicago, 1929; L. Wirth, *The Ghetto*, Chicago, 1928.

against fragmentation there has been an increasing concern with interdisciplinary research and with the intellectual sterility which results from breakdowns of communication between specialists. A recent book by Kamarovsky[1] lists some of the major kinds of interdisciplinary convergences which have occurred:

1. Where empirical data in one field can be illuminated by concepts from another. For example, Neil Smelser, a sociologist, has applied concepts developed by Talcott Parsons and others to the study of the industrial revolution in eighteenth-century Britain.[2]

2. Concepts and hypotheses in one field may stimulate research in another. In our discussion of Herbert Spencer's work we noted the utilization of biological concepts and the fact that such concepts have continued to stimulate sociologists up to the present day; prominent among them is the notion of evolution.

3. Two disciplines may bring their respective theoretical frameworks to bear on the same empirical problem, e.g. industrial sociologists and economists have collaborated in the study of labour–management relations.

4. A method developed in one discipline may be usefully adopted in another. Russell Planck, for example, has shown how the public opinion survey can be used to clarify historical generalizations in modern times.[3]

We cannot discuss the interaction between sociology and all relevant disciplines, so we have selected economics, political science and history for special attention.[4] Before doing so, however, it may be useful to give a few brief definitions of other

[1] M. Kamarovsky, ed., *Common Frontiers of the Social Sciences*, Free Press, 1957.

[2] N. Smelser, *Social Change in the Industrial Revolution*, London, Routledge & Kegan Paul, 1959.

[3] R. Planck, Public opinion in France after the liberation, 1944–49, in Kamarovsky, *op. cit.*, p.184.

[4] For a general discussion of sociology in relation to these and other disciplines, see J. Gillin, ed., *For a Science of Social Man*, New York, Macmillan, 1954.

disciplines or sub-disciplines whose subject matter overlaps with sociology.[1] In most cases the definitions by specialists of their own field range from broad to narrow conceptions; we have selected the definitions having the widest acceptance but where in doubt have favoured narrow interpretations.

*Social anthropology* is probably the most difficult to differentiate from sociology of any discipline considered here. Most of its practitioners, if asked to do so, would point to traditional interests rather than to any difference in theoretical objectives or in subject matter. Among these traditional concerns is the concentration on small, pre-literate societies and the reliance on direct, participant observation over long periods. British anthropology has been particularly interested in the kinship structures of pre-literate societies. In spite of this traditional orientation, few anthropologists would be prepared to exclude large-scale, modern societies from their sphere of interest and in actual studies of this kind the borderline between the two subjects becomes very tenuous.

*Ethnology* overlaps with social anthropology in many definitions but attempts have been made to define it as the study of culture rather than social structure. In practice such an artificial boundary is impossible to maintain. French and German ethnologists confine its subject matter exclusively to pre-literate societies in an attempt to maintain the independent status of the subject.

*Ethnography* is distinctive in that it refers to the *descriptive* recording of culture in pre-literate societies; it is not concerned with analytical generalization or theory.

*Demography* is concerned with changes in population produced by births, deaths and migration, also with the stratification of populations into sub-groupings according to such criteria as age, sex, marital status and country of origin. Its methods are essentially quantitative and statistical but, increasingly, there is a concern with psychological and sociological factors underlying such phenomena as differential birth rates between sub-groupings and decisions regarding geographical movement.

[1] The definitions are taken from J. Gould and W. Kolb, eds., *A Dictionary of the Social Sciences*, London, Tavistock Publications, 1964.

*Human ecology* has already been described as the study of relationships between populations and their physical–economic environments.

*Criminology* and *Penology* are concerned with formulating generalizations about the development of criminal law, why people break laws, how criminals are dealt with and the effects of particular modes of treatment.

*Social psychology* is concerned with the formation and modification of the "self" or personality through interaction with others. It differs from psychology in emphasizing the socio-cultural context of thinking, feeling and perceiving rather than upon these processes as universal human phenomena.

Among modern disciplines developed under the stimulus of the computer we may point to *Cybernetics* as having a special relevance to sociology.[1] This is a particular approach to the study of organisms and machines which emphasizes (a) the self-maintenance or self-regulation of organic or mechanical systems through *feedback*, i.e. the process by which information concerning the state of the system is produced by the system itself and leads to automatic adjustment, and (b) the communication of information within the system.

## History and Sociology

In recent years there has been a movement amongst American scholars to revitalize historical sociology, and this has been documented by Cahnman and Boskoff.[2] As a preliminary definition of the boundary between history and sociology, we may cite their contrast between the historian's interest in sequences of action focused upon individuals and the sociologist's concern with institutionalized patterns of behaviour performed by social actors. Sociologists have used historical data in the study of long-term social change,[3] but have often failed to recognize the necessity

[1] See N. Wiener, *Cybernetics*, New York, John Wiley, 1949.

[2] W. Cahnman and A. Boskoff, eds., *Sociology and History: Theory and Research*, Free Press, 1964.

[3] For example, S. Eisenstadt, *The Political Systems of Empires*, Free Press, 1963.

of a historical perspective in empirical studies of contemporary society. This is illustrated in a recent article by Stephan Thernstrom on the "perils of historical naiveté".[1] Taking Lloyd Warner's *Yankee City* studies as his subject, Thernstrom describes the errors which resulted from misconceptions about the community's history. For example, Warner developed a theory of blocked mobility based upon the contention that in the expanding frontier towns of the early nineteenth century the economic craft structure had provided avenues of social mobility for the lower classes. He thought that the spread of the factory system had largely blocked these avenues. He concluded that Newburyport (this being the real name of the town) must expect "revolutionary outbreaks expressing frustrated aspirations". It was in the context of this theory that Warner interpreted a strike in 1933 which closed all the shoe factories in the town. He saw it as being too radical a departure from the communal tradition of peaceful labour relations to be understood merely as an economic phenomenon. According to Warner's reconstruction of the past, every working-class youngster became an apprentice to an independent master craftsman and after skilled training probably became a master himself. Workers and masters shared common values and interacted freely at a personal level; the craftsman had self-respect and social class differences in the community were negligible. With the coming of the machine and the factory system, however, the skilled worker lost his self-respect and his economic function; mobility was blocked and social cohesion shaken. In the shoe industry ownership became vested in absentee factory owners and the workers in self-defence formed a union. In this way a class division on Marxian lines appeared.

On the basis of his own research as a professional historian Thernstrom argues that the open community of skilled craftsmen never in fact existed. It was a communal myth relayed to Warner by elderly respondents of the upper middle class. There was a craft order in the very early nineteenth century, but its outstanding

[1] S. Thernstrom, Yankee city revisited, *American Sociological Review*, **30** (Apr. 1965), 234.

features were a religiously-sanctioned ruling *élite* and a deferential lower class. This had disappeared long before the end of the century and had been replaced by factory production without any manifestations of frustrated aspiration or working-class solidarity. Production was highly mechanized in the shoe industry before 1880 and control had already passed largely into the hands of absentee owners. During this period there was no evidence that labour relations were better in locally owned firms than in firms controlled from outside. In both cases predominantly Irish-Catholic employees were concerned with wringing financial concessions from Yankee-Protestant mill-owners. The theory of blocked mobility is criticized as being based upon an inadequate knowledge of the past and certainly unnecessary to explain the strike of 1933.

## Political Science and Sociology

The subject matter of political science (i.e. politics) may be defined as the "processes of human action by which conflict concerning, on the one hand, the common good and, on the other hand, the interests of groups is carried on or settled, always involving the use of, or struggle for, power".[1] The emphasis of this definition upon human interaction reflects a fairly recent shift of interest by political scientists from traditional topics such as the theory of the State, the mechanics of government and the formal organization of public administration, towards the study of political behaviour as manifested in such diverse phenomena as voting, decision-making, opinion formation and pressure-group strategy.[2] Associated with this shift of interest there has been an increasing theoretical emphasis on the analysis of political systems, i.e. the channels of recruitment to political positions, the way roles are performed in various types of structure, political norms and values, and many other topics which have been touched

[1] Gould and Kolb, *op. cit.*, under Politics.
[2] See Heinz Elau, *Recent Developments in the Behavioural Study of Politics*, Stanford University Press, 1961.

on in our discussion of sociology. Given the concern with political behaviour and with conflict as an integral part of such behaviour it is not surprising that the system models developed by political scientists lay more emphasis on function than on structure. We shall return to the discussion of one or two such models in the next chapter.

Complementing the shift in political science towards behavioural studies there has been a growing interest within sociology in political phenomena. Apart from the topics already mentioned in connection with political scientists there has been an impressive development of research in the area of local community power structures.

In the analysis of whole societies, i.e. macrosociology, there has been a constant interplay between the study of social class and the study of power. A central idea in this interplay has been that of class conflict. As described by Marx this was a revolutionary force inherent in pre-Communist society. Subsequent reformulations have placed the emphasis on competing interest groups seeking limited ends within agreed limits. In fact there are doubts as to whether the Marxian concept of social class is relevant to the conflict groups of societies which have developed beyond the *laissez-faire* capitalism of nineteenth-century Europe.[1]

Another important element in political sociology is centred around the concept of *mass society*.[2] The term refers to a particular model of modern society characterized by an emphasis on the impersonal, bureaucratized relationships which have developed as large-scale organizations come to dominate society and the consequent destruction of primary group ties and loyalties. The breakdown of primary ties to the family, the local community and so on leads to feelings of detachment or alienation amongst individuals. At the political level it leaves people open to manipulation by *élites* who dominate bureaucratic organizations and the

[1] For an elaboration of this point, see Ralf Dahrendorf, *Class and Class Conflict in Industrial Society*, Stanford University Press, 1958.

[2] See, for example, W. Kornhauser, *The Politics of Mass Society*, Free Press, 1959.

mass media of communication. Anti-democratic mass movements such as fascism or communism offer substitute loyalties to the alienated, unorganized masses in order to gain power. Once there they can maintain control through large-scale organization as well as through propaganda. The theory grew up as part of a moral, emotional and intellectual reaction against Nazism and Stalinism. A recognition of its ideological biases should not, however, detract from the contributions its adherents have made to social science.[1]

### Economics and Sociology

The definition of economics given in Gould and Kolb's *Dictionary of the Social Sciences* is that it is "the study of human behaviour as it relates scarce means, which have alternative uses, to given ends such as the maximization of income, usually employing price data in the comparison". It uses quantitative price and market models as basic conceptual frameworks. The empirical interplay between economics and sociology begins where prediction based upon purely economic factors fails, i.e. where non-economic factors such as attitudes, values and group loyalties have to be introduced. There are phenomena such as the level of confidence in the business community, the tendency of trade unions to indulge in "non-rational" strikes and the proclivity of consumers to indulge in economically irrational behaviour which have forced economists to consider non-economic factors. One manifestation of this is the increased use being made of questionnaire surveys by economists to study consumers and producers.[2]

Lack of space prevents any broad survey of the empirical and theoretical convergences which have occurred between economics and sociology. We would merely draw attention to one particularly important area of empirical convergence.

[1] For a critique of the theory, see J. Gusfield, Mass society and extremist politics, *American Sociological Review*, **27** (Feb. 1962), 19.

[2] See Katona, The function of survey research in economics, in Kamarovsky, *op. cit.*

Within the field of industrial sociology, there has grown up a special school of thought which has been given the rather ambiguous title of "plant" sociology.[1] "Plant" refers to units of economic organization such as the factory or shop. The main figure in developing this school was Elton Mayo and its greatest achievement was the series of Hawthorne studies referred to in the previous chapter. The "plant" sociologist sees the industrial enterprise as a community rather than as an association of self-interested economic actors. Thus the manager is evaluated in terms of the social cohesion and communal spirit that exists in a given enterprise rather than in terms of its productive efficiency, although the two are closely associated. This conception of the managerial role is far removed from that of the orthodox economist who saw it as allocating and combining scarce resources in a more or less free market. In practice it means emphasizing the informal small group and its leaders rather than the formal organization, both from the point of view of managerial functioning and of empirical research. As in the case of "mass society", there is an evaluative bias in favour of the primary group. It is assumed that man needs to be rooted in such groups, in work as in other areas of society, in order to achieve a full, satisfying life. Kerr and Fisher make many searching criticisms of the school, but give credit for the light which it has thrown upon such problems as absenteeism, high labour turnover, inefficiency and unofficial strikes.

[1] Kerr and Fisher, Plant sociology, in Kamarovsky, *op. cit.*, p. 281.

CHAPTER 4

# SOME INSTITUTIONAL AREAS
# OF SOCIETY

WE STATED in a previous chapter that all societies face basic problems related to the satisfaction of human needs, adjustment to the environment and the maintenance of orderly social interaction. The positions and roles developed in meeting these recurring and universal problems form distinctive clusters of normatively regulated interaction which are often referred to as *social institutions*. As the term institution is also used to refer to specific organizations of persons such as schools, hospitals and prisons, there are certain ambiguities involved in talking about social institutions and we shall talk instead of *institutionalized areas of interaction*. In this chapter we shall discuss three such areas: the economy, the polity and the family. The first two are of course the province of specialized social sciences, but in each case there is a considerable interdisciplinary overlap with sociology. This is due partly to a common concern with explaining human behaviour and partly to the distinctively sociological concern with analysing the whole of society as a coherent system of interdependent parts.

## THE ECONOMY

Within the framework of the whole social system of a society the economy may be conceptualized as a particular sub-system of roles and activities focused around problems of adaptation to the physical environment.[1] These problems include not only the

[1] This approach has been most fully developed in the work of Talcott Parsons (see T. Parsons, *The Social System*, Free Press, 1952).

satisfaction of individual needs for food, clothing and shelter but also the production of resources for attaining collective goals such as defence, education and social welfare. It should be noted that in referring to individual needs we include not only the biological requisites for survival but also culturally defined wants and expectations. In an affluent society these may include such things as owning a car, purchasing a house, sending children to college or having central heating. Such social needs vary according to the general standard of living achieved in a society and according to the position of a person within it. The important point is that they are perceived as needs or justifiable wants by individuals and failure to meet them can result in threats to the stability of the social system.

Within the economic sub-system roles and activities are organized into clearly defined patterns governed by rules and norms, i.e. they are institutionalized. In our own society this is most clearly seen in the existence of specialized units for the production of goods and services such as factories, mines, banks and shipyards. As we noted in an earlier chapter, the study of such units is the special concern of what has been called "plant" sociology. This in turn is one branch of a broader sub-discipline called industrial sociology; this being concerned with such topics as choice of occupations, the development of careers, adjustment to work, satisfaction with work and occupational prestige as well as with the organization of economic units.

In conceptualizing the economy as a sub-system of society we draw attention to the fact that it is merely one of several sub-systems and to the associated problem of specifying the "boundary" relationships between them. The problem is too difficult to deal with in an introductory text but we can indicate some of the interactions which occur.[1]

Interaction with the political sub-system occurs where the economy provides the resources for attaining politically defined goals such as military strength, the provision of old age pensions,

[1] For a sophisticated treatment of the problem see T. Parsons and N. Smelser, *Economy and Society*, Free Press, 1956.

and universal education. The polity in turn reacts upon the economy through controlling the creation of liquid funds by such means as interest rates or credit facilities. The interaction between these two sub-systems has become a subject of great interest in the context of the modern conception of the planned economy.

Interaction also occurs with the other institutionalized area of society dealt with in this chapter, viz. the family. The household purchases goods and services produced in the economic sector and in turn supplies labour services essential to further production. The reciprocal flow of inputs and outputs at this boundary is mediated largely through the payment of wages.

A rather different way of conceptualizing the relationship between the economy and society is to adopt a historical or developmental perspective and concentrate on social change instead of social cohesion. Students in this area have devoted much attention to analysing the transition from simple to complex economies both in terms of the social preconditions for economic advancement and in terms of its consequences for society.

In primitive societies economic activity is almost entirely devoted to satisfying the biological requirements for survival. Where men are able to move beyond the stage of subsistence, mainly through discovering more efficient ways of performing the primary functions of feeding, clothing and sheltering themselves, more time and effort can be devoted to producing tools and other kinds of capital equipment which are not themselves directly consumable but which contribute to the more efficient production of need-satisfying consumer goods. In late eighteenth-century Britain the invention of mechanized capital equipment driven by steam-power gave such an impetus to the productivity of labour that the period has been characterized as one of revolution, i.e. the Industrial Revolution. Since then productivity has been dramatically increased by the systematic application of scientific knowledge to economic activity. Some societies have attained a level of affluence where the major problem is that of increasing demand by creating new wants, rather than of how to supply more goods. The historic process of development from the subsistence economy to the affluent society has been conceptualized by W. Rostow as proceeding through several distinct stages.[1]

*Stage* 1. This is the subsistence level achieved by pre-literate or "primitive" societies. It is characterized by a high concentration on agriculture and consequent restriction on geographical mobility which is reflected in the social sphere by an almost complete absence of change. The attitude towards economic production is non-technological, i.e. there is a reliance on rule-of-thumb procedures handed down from the past. Attempts to control the environment take the form of magic rather than the systematic application of reason. Because of these factors there is an inherent limit on the level of attainable output.

*Stage* 2. When scientific thought develops and begins to be applied to practical problems, either through conquest, imitation or internal processes, then the preconditions for "take-off" exist. (This is a more general and distinctively American term for what has been called the industrial revolution.) At this stage, economic growth is seen by certain people as an end in itself as well as a means of attaining other ends. They are motivated to invest money for profit in manufacturing, commerce and trade.[2] The entrepreneur must, to some extent, be free from the attitudinal and social restraints of traditional society; he is part product and part agent of social change. Associated with the development of entrepreneurial activity is the centralization of political power. This enables economic activity to proceed within a framework of law and order as well as providing a concentration of power which may be used in a directive way to stimulate economic growth. This occurred in nineteenth-century France and may be observed today in many of the developing nations.

*Stage* 3. When the emerging forces of change become predominant and economic growth is cumulative, then the crucial "take-off" stage is reached. In general terms the successful completion of this

[1] W. Rostow, *Stages of Economic Growth*, Cambridge, Mass., 1960.
[2] For an attempt to explain this motivation, see Max Weber, *The Protestant Ethic and the Spirit of Capitalism*, London, Allen & Unwin, 1930.

stage requires: (a) a "surplus" of consumer goods to support those occupied in producing capital equipment and in running services such as transportation, finance and distribution; (b) technological development based upon scientific discovery as an institutionalized element of the economy; (c) active political encouragement and financial aid. Some kinds of capital equipment such as roads, schools, public health services and so on require high initial investment with little or no financial return. The profit motive being inadequate to provide for such things, there must be deliberate political participation in investment.

The practical problem at this stage, according to Rostow, is to reach and sustain a rate of capital investment amounting to some 10 per cent of the national income, at the same time utilizing technological advances to ensure that each extra unit of investment increases the volume of output by about three units. The huge amounts of capital investment needed to make the transition to industrialism may be obtained in three basic ways:

1. By forced saving, as in the entrepreneurial exploitation of labour characteristic of early capitalism, or in the governmental exploitation of labour characteristic of early communism in Russia, and impatient nationalism in parts of contemporary Africa, Asia and South America.
2. By voluntary saving as in stock exchange investment or the cultivation of abstinence as a moral duty.
3. By obtaining aid from other societies in the form of investment, credit facilities or ready-made capital equipment (including skilled workers).

*Stage* 4. At this stage, called "the drive to maturity", some 10 to 20 per cent of the national income is regularly invested so that economic growth outstrips the inevitable growth of population as the standard of living rises. The economy is then able to move beyond its dependence on a few industries based upon indigenous natural resources and produce anything made possible by technological development. There is a diversification of industry to meet the demands of international competition.

*Stage* 5. This is the stage of "high mass-consumption" reached by the United States, Canada, Australia, New Zealand and some Western European countries. Increased efficiency permits a decreasing number of workers to satisfy primary needs and the occupational structure shifts increasingly to the production of "non-essential" consumer goods and services for a mass market. The problem at this stage is one of abundance and may be solved in several ways. One solution is for the government to soak up an increasing proportion of private income and invest it in preparation for war, exploration of outer space, aid to underdeveloped countries, the provision of social welfare services and so on. Another solution is for the producers of goods and services to persuade people to spend more money. In the context of mass-consumption, advertising may be seen as a necessary means of maintaining the balance of supply and demand rather than as an iniquitous way of persuading people to spend money they cannot afford. Just as in earlier stages the application of the natural sciences to production was a necessary condition for growth, so in this stage it may be argued that the application of the human sciences to demand is necessary for further growth. Sociologists and psychologists are employed in growing numbers to staff market research and advertising departments.

The transition to affluence is in its way as revolutionary as the earlier transition to industrialism. There is a similar pressure placed upon established values and institutions, accompanied by the appearance of new personality types demanding freedom from the past, and creating new life-styles geared to the opportunities and demands of a changing social environment.

Clearly the study of economic growth is of crucial importance in the analysis of social change, but it is necessary to specify as far as possible the way in which particular economic arrangements encourage, limit or are associated with particular arrangements in other institutionalized areas such as the family, education, religion or politics. Only in this way can we move from historical generalizations, summarizing changes in particular societies, to abstract propositions about social systems generally. Students of the newly developing nations have been particularly concerned with establishing relationships between economic conditions and other social phenomena. One example of this work is the attempt to specify the relationship between level of economic development and the existence of stable democratic government. Some studies emphasize the problem of how far democratic government is compatible with politically enforced industrialization. Others are more concerned with elaborating the economic conditions which make democratic government possible. An article by Seymour Lipset illustrates the latter approach.[1]

Lipset gives a working definition of democracy as a political system supplying regular constitutional opportunities for changing the government by allowing the population to choose between alternative sets of policy-makers. He then defines a number of geographical-cultural areas and within each area classifies nations as being high or low in democratic attributes. These nations are then compared on a wide range of socio-economic variables in order to isolate uniform associations between democratic government and socio-economic conditions. One of his findings was that highly democratic nations within each area were strikingly higher on *per capita* income, level of industrialization, urbanization and literacy than those low on democratic attributes. Data within particular nations supported the conclusion that the most important single factor associated with democratic government was the general level of education. Lipset suggests that increased income, economic security and education permit people to develop longer time perspectives and greater tolerance in their political orientations. In this way greater allowance is made for the possibility of alternative solutions to problems and the emotional pressure for immediate, dramatic action is relieved. This is merely one plausible line of explanation in accounting for observed associations between socio-economic conditions and political arrangements.

The social psychological implications of economic insecurity are of interest not only in comparing the political systems of different

[1] S. Lipset, chap. II, New York, Doubleday, 1960.

societies, but also in explaining the differences in political behaviour which occur between social strata within a single society. It is generally accepted on the basis of historical evidence that the transitions to industrialism in Europe during the nineteenth century involved considerable economic insecurity for large sections of the population and an associated hostility between the owners of the means of production and the working classes. As the standard of living improved and the insecurity declined, so there was a disappearance of the political unrest which prompted Marx to predict the inevitable destruction of capitalism by revolution.

In fact, capitalism, as Marx observed it, has disappeared; but the process has been effected by means not envisaged by him. The confrontation between owner-managers and workers has been greatly complicated and consequently divested of revolutionary potential by far-reaching changes in property ownership, the structure of industry and the kind of work people do. The growth of joint stock companies produced the phenomenon of the separation of ownership and control in industry. Ownership has increasingly becomed vested in shareholders taking little interest in anything but the profitability of companies, whereas control has become the function of a professional managerial class differing from the early capitalist entrepreneurs in training, skills and attitudes towards employees. The ownership of property is still highly concentrated but the exercise of control over it has been largely delegated to specialists. As the former capitalist class changed, so on the labour side of industry there were comparable processes of differentiation. Many of these can be traced to technological developments demanding new skills and making traditional skills obsolete. At the turn of the twentieth century there was the development of a semi-skilled stratum posing a threat to the status and security of skilled workers and achieving a higher standard of living than was possible for unskilled workers. More recently the bargaining power of trade unions and the concern of managers for good industrial relations have contributed to the increasing affluence of the working classes. In Chapter 1 we referred to the process of "embourgeoisement" as one consequence or manifestation of working class affluence.

The shift in the economic system from the production of consumer and capital goods to the provision of services has not only affected the existing occupational structure but has created a whole new stratum of employees in offices, shops and so on which can hardly be termed a class in any sense other than being a category of persons sharing a similar style of life. Certainly it is difficult to see them as constituting a social class in the Marxian sense of a potentially cohesive political force.

Ralf Dahrendorf argues that the economic system of capitalism described by Marx and other nineteenth-century writers is merely one particular form of what he calls industrial society.[1] This broader type of system is characterized by economic rationalism, mechanized factory production, market exchange and other necessary concomitants of industrial production. It is not necessarily characterized by class conflict or even by social classes in the Marxian sense.

While it may be agreed that socio-economic changes in our own society have largely invalidated the class conflict model, it must not be assumed that the concept of social class has been made irrelevant. The fact remains that people can be classified according to occupational prestige, income, education or other closely associated indicators of social status and that such classifications are not merely statistical categories but reflect differences in values, goals, attitudes and behaviour. For example, high social status is associated with greater political involvement, with more favourable attitudes towards further education and with a more rational mode of decision-making in such situations as occupational choice.[2]

Although much of the work dealing with the effects of work experiences and occupational demands on individuals concentrates on social class differences, this is not the only aspect of

[1] R. Dahrendorf, *Class and Class Conflict in Industrial Society*, Stanford University Press, 1958.

[2] For a discussion of some of these generalizations, see H. Hyman, The value systems of different classes, in R. Bendix and S. Lipset, eds., *Class, Status and Power*, p. 426, Free Press, 1953.

sociological interest. One of the outstanding characteristics of modern industrial society is the extent to which individuals are required to play roles within the context of bureaucratic organizations. It is therefore of sociological interest to find out whether the mere fact of being involved in such organizations tends to produce characteristic types of attitude and behaviour. One of the best-known contributions to this area of study is an essay by Robert Merton on the personality characteristics encouraged in bureaucratic officials.[1] Among the points made by Merton are the following:

(a) The successful operation of a bureaucracy demands that the behaviour of officials be highly reliable and predictable; there are therefore sanctions encouraging a self-disciplined conformity to official regulations.

(b) Appropriate attitudes of obedience to authority and conformity to regulations are so important to the organization that pressures to adopt them go beyond merely technical considerations of efficiency, i.e. there is a safety-margin in the degree of pressure exerted. One consequence of this is that adherence to rules becomes valued as an end in itself rather than as a means of attaining organizational goals. This is manifested as the familiar "red-tape" mentality. The devices for ensuring predictability of performance may be over-effective in the sense of leading to timidity and habitual conservatism.

(c) One of the defining characteristics of a bureaucracy is that regulations are applied impersonally without consideration for special relationships or emotional factors. In dealing with the clientele of an organization the same impersonal application of rules gives us an appearance of insensitivity or even inhumanity to official behaviour. Whether the appearance reflects a real personality trait or is merely a projection of hostility on the part of the clients is a matter for empirical research.

[1] R. K. Merton, *Social Theory and Social Structure*, pp. 151–160, Free Press, 1949.

While Merton is concerned with the personality traits of bureaucratic officials as they are manifested in the work situation, there is a suggestion that more deeply rooted personality factors may be involved, e.g. a generalized attitude of submission to authority which would appear in other areas of behaviour. A recent example of research concerned with the psychological implications of work experiences is an analysis by Robert Blauner of job attitudes in four different industries.[1] The four industries were craft printing, textile manufacturing, automobile manufacturing and chemical production. Blauner analysed the responses of 3000 manual workers, looking for evidence of alienation. Alienation was defined as a set of related attitudes to the social environment rather than as a single attitude. The set includes feelings of meaninglessness, feelings of powerlessness to control the social environment, feelings of non-belonging and conscious self-estrangement from society.[2]  Blauner draws several conclusions from his comparison of workers in different industries; the following are indicative. The craft printers were found to be particularly low in signs of alienation. Blauner explains this in terms of the printers' higher satisfaction in the performance of a skilled trade plus the fact of having a craft monopoly permitting greater control over working conditions. The greater alienation shown by the textile workers is explained in terms of their physical isolation in the mechanized work organization of the cotton mill. There were alleviating factors in this industry based upon the integration of textile workers into closely-knit communities, which provided some feelings of social belonging and a meaningful existence. The most alienated workers were those in the automobile industry; their work was the least meaningful in personal terms, the most insecure and the least amenable to personal control. The pattern and rhythm of work is dictated by the assembly line and there is little room for personal deviation from the

---

[1] R. Blauner, *Alienation and Freedom: The Factory Worker and His Industry*, University of Chicago, 1964.

[2] These were taken from an article by M. Seeman, On the Meaning of Alienation, *American Sociological Review*, **24** (Dec. 1959), 783.

dictates of mechanized mass-production. Blauner suggests that the extent to which the individual can control the pace and quality of his work is an important factor in determining whether or not he develops generalized feelings of alienation.

Some studies of the personal implications of work focus on communities rather than individuals. These are usually small, stable communities based upon a single industry such as coal-mining, fishing or ship-building where the work is highly salient in the way of life. Work defines the identity of such communities for its residents and pervades the whole way of life rather than being a particular aspect of it. Many primitive societies are of this kind but there are studies of work communities in modern society. An example is the study by Dennis, Henriques and Slaughter of an English coal-mining village.[1] One of the major themes of the study is the importance of the danger involved in the work in the creation of strong ties of friendship and mutual aid. These ties are reflected in the social life of the community as well as the mine. During their leisure hours the men seek relief from the tensions of work in each other's company and form all-male peer groups to undertake masculine activities such as drinking and attending football matches. The ties are also reflected in the strongly cohesive union organization of the miners.

## THE POLITY

In this section we shall attempt to distinguish political inter-action as a particular area of social behaviour and indicate the way in which the polity may be studied as a particular system of roles and activities.

The basis of human society is that its members co-operate in order to satisfy their various needs and goals. In so far as valued resources are scarce relative to the demands of individuals there will be disagreement over their allocation. Some authoritative agency is therefore required in order to resolve disputes and to

[1] N. Dennis, F. Henriques and C. Slaughter, *Coal Is Our Life*, London, Eyre & Spottiswoode, 1956.

make decisions regarding the allocation of resources in society. Included in the latter function is the definition of collective goals and priorities. Certain positions must be established with a legitimate monopoly of the means of physical coercion, these are institutionalized as governments or political authorities and constitute one crucial element of the political system. We stress the word "legitimate" in order to point out that political interaction centres around the *authoritative* allocation of resources, i.e. the allocation is typically considered to be binding by the members of society in terms of agreed rules and values. No political system could survive on the basis of force alone. The motivation for according legitimacy to a political system may be self-interest, loyalty, tradition or moral belief but without it there can be no social order.

The more complex a society becomes the more difficult it is to make decisions regarding priorities and goal-attainment. For this reason there is a historical tendency for policy-making to become a specialized, full-time activity performed through permanent political organizations. It should be noted, however, that even in the most complex societies there are non-political means of resolving disputes and allocating resources. In our own society there is considerable room for the settlement of disputes between individuals or groups without political intervention, e.g. collective bargaining between unions and employers. Similarly the allocation of resources occurs largely through exchanges in "free" markets, regulated by supply and demand rather than through political authority. In both cases the actual degree of political control depends upon ideology as well as upon considerations of efficiency or situational demands.

In the preceding remarks and in the section generally we are concentrating on political activity as it occurs *within* a society, i.e. upon internal political functions. In doing this we are following the major emphasis of current sociological theory. One danger of this emphasis is that it obscures the significance of political activity *between* societies, i.e. the external functions of formulating foreign policy, ensuring military security and maximizing control in the international sphere. The mobilization of resources into effective power is not confined to ensuring internal social order, it is also used to further national interests. In order for a nation to establish an identity and a respected place in world affairs it must interact with other nations and attempt to create a desired impression of itself. While the tendency for nations, or more accurately the individuals representing them, to maximize prestige and influence may be accepted as an empirical generalization, the explanation of why this should be so is very difficult in general theoretical terms. International affairs receive considerable attention in contemporary social science but studies in this area are rather divorced from the mainstream of theory and research in political sociology.

There have been many attempts to construct theoretical models of the political system but we shall concentrate on a particular approach sometimes referred to as "whole systems analysis", which has emerged recently as an important focus of theoretical and empirical effort. It is an attempt to provide a conceptual scheme for ordering and analysing data from widely varying societies and thereby permitting the comparative study of political systems.

One of the most prominent exponents of system analysis in political science is David Easton and his work provides a useful starting point in describing the approach.[1] Easton sees the political system as being basically concerned with the making and execution of authoritative decisions. In elaborating his scheme he adopts the cybernetic notion of a system which transforms inputs into outputs, the latter being fed back into the system to keep it going. The raw materials or *inputs* of the political system are of two kinds: (a) conflicting *demands* by persons and groups who cannot all be satisfied; (b) dispositions towards particular kinds of co-operation which are called *supports*. Through such transformation processes as the formation of interest groups, the

[1] See D. Easton, *The Political System*, New York, Alfred Knopf, 1953; also *A Framework for Political Analysis*, Englewood Cliffs, New Jersey, Prentice-Hall, 1965.

activity of political parties and legislation these inputs are converted into authoritative decisions or *outputs*.

The supports forming part of the input factor may be of a *diffuse* kind, e.g. feelings of patriotism, beliefs in democratic rights or habits of obedience to authority, or they may be *specific*, e.g. satisfaction with the standard of living. The former are the product of political socialization and form part of the general culture of a society. The latter are reflections of satisfaction with the outputs of the political system, i.e. with the rewards and benefits produced by the policies of those in authority. The idea of input and output has been utilized by two other prominent political scientists, Gabriel Almond and James Coleman, in elaborating a conceptual scheme.[1] We give its main elements in some detail because the scheme has been widely used in empirical research, particularly in studies of the developing nations.

The input functions are defined as follows:

1. *Political socialization and recruitment*. Socialization is a process of learning whereby common attitudes, values and beliefs are created in the members of a society; political socialization is a particular element of the process. The recruitment process is a continuation of socialization in that it fashions people into political role-players, e.g. voters, party organizers, Members of Parliament or civil servants.

2. *Interest articulation*. The main element here is the formation of particular groups and associations to put forward specific demands to those in authority. It also includes, however, latent interest articulation whereby demands are communicated by relatively unspecified means such as non-voting, migration to other countries or protest marches. The importance of political commentators in the press, on radio or television lies partly in their ability to interpret such behavioural cues and give them verbal articulation.

3. *Interest aggregation*. This differs from articulation in being a more inclusive combination of interests forming a coherent

[1] G. Almond and J. Coleman, *The Politics of the Developing Areas*, Princeton, 1960.

policy rather than a series of specific demands. In our own society this function is performed by political parties but in other societies it may be performed by tribal, racial or religious groupings. In these cases, however, there is a greater likelihood that politically soluble disputes over the allocation of resources will become entangled with broader social issues, producing a basic cleavage between social groupings rather than a confined conflict of interests. Where political disputes follow lines of difference drawn on racial, religious or ideological grounds then interest aggregation becomes a threat to social cohesion rather than a convenient arrangement for transforming demands into policies.

4. *Political communication.* This function is carried on through speeches, conversations, television interviews, political meetings and so on. It centres around the flow of communication between governors and the governed. If the governors themselves control this function then one has the phenomenon of propaganda.

The *output* functions of the political system are described by Almond and Coleman as follows:—

1. *Rule-making*, which is most clearly exemplified in the work of such legislative bodies as the Houses of Parliament.
2. *Rule application*, which refers to the process by which authoritative decisions are implemented. In our own society this function is performed through administrative bureaucracies staffed by civil servants.
3. *Rule adjudication*, through which disputes over the meaning or interpretation of rules are resolved. One of the main principles of democratic political systems is that the judiciary be independent of legislative and executive bodies.

The above scheme is intended only as a descriptive model of the political system but the student may find it useful as a framework within which to organize further reading on political institutions and political behaviour. References to such reading were given in the preceding chapter in the section on political science and sociology.

## MARRIAGE AND THE FAMILY

Human beings, in comparison with other animal species, undergo a long period of biological immaturity during which their physical survival depends upon the readiness of others to supply their needs. During this period they also have to be taught to function as social beings, i.e. they must be socialized. All societies have institutionalized arrangements to ensure that these two functions are performed. These arrangements differ considerably in detail but always include the legitimation of reproduction through *marriage*; culturally defined *kinship* relations; and social groupings based upon the rules of descent, i.e. kinship groups. The family is the most basic, and in our society the most common type of kinship group.

Marriage has been defined by Westermarck as "a relation of one or more men to one or more women, which is recognized by custom or law, and involves certain rights or duties both in the case of the parties entering the union and in the case of the children born into it".[1] The quotation draws particular attention to the function of marriage in ensuring that children will be the responsibility of designated persons. As Bredemeier and Stephenson point out the principle of legitimacy is particularly important in establishing a tie of responsibility between a child and an adult male.[2] While the tie with an adult female is readily visible this is not the case with a male, and fatherhood must be clearly defined in social terms so as to reduce the danger of non-responsible procreation. In fact the social father is usually the biological father but this need not be the case, even ignoring the possibility of cuckoldry. In some primitive societies, for example, a woman's brothers may be required to undertake the duties of fatherhood.

Westermarck's definition also draws attention to variations in the number of partners involved in the marriage contract. The

---

[1] E. Westermarck, *The History of Human Marriage*, London, Macmillan, 1921.

[2] H. Bredemeier and R. Stephenson, *The Analysis of Social Systems*, New York, Holt, Rinehart & Winston, 1962.

most common type, in primitive and modern societies, is one husband and one wife, i.e. *monogamy*, but plural mating, i.e. *polygamy*, is also a widespread practice. In many cases this arrangement is necessary to ensure a sufficient birth-rate due to a shortage of either men or women. Of the two forms which polygamy may take *polygyny* (one husband with more than one wife) is more common than *polyandry* (one wife with more than one husband). George Murdock's comparative study of 238 societies showed that 193 permitted polygyny, 43 monogamy and only 2 polyandry.[1] Although the figures seem to indicate that polygamy is more common than monogamy, in practice monogamy is more frequent even where other forms of marriage are permitted, due to the economic problems of maintaining a large household and to the fact that the sexes are usually equally balanced. Further, many societies characterized by polygamy have small populations.

In many pre-literate and non-industrialized societies marriages are arranged by parents as part of an exchange of property or a joining together of kinship groups for mutual advantage. Some element of arrangement occurs in our own society as in the case of royal marriages or arrangements between business dynasties. At a more general level parents generally attempt to ensure that their children, particularly females, only come into contact with socially desirable mates. This is reflected in the choice of "suitable" residential areas as well as in such customs as inviting potential in-laws to tea. Whatever economic or social factors may be involved, however, there is usually a sincere attempt in all societies to match couples temperamentally suited to one another. Ralph Linton, the American anthropologist, states that "many societies believe that the parents have better judgement in such matters, but very few of them approve of the forcing of children into unions which are actively distasteful to them".[2]

Apart from the preferences of individuals or parents for desirable mates there are other factors which may influence the

---

[1] G. Murdock, *Social Structure*, p. 28, New York, Macmillan, 1949.
[2] R. Linton, *The Study of Man*, p. 174, New York, Appleton–Century–Crofts, 1936.

choice of marital partner. In some societies there exists the practice of *exogamy* whereby a person in a given kinship grouping is required to choose a partner from another specified kinship grouping; in other societies the choice is restricted to persons within the same kinship grouping, this is termed *endogamy* and is often linked to the idea of preserving the purity of status of a group. There also exist specific rules concerning re-marriage in several societies. The *levirate* is a rule whereby a widow is expected to marry a brother of the dead husband; the *sororate* conversely requires that a widower marries a sister of his dead wife.

One other aspect of marriage which we must consider is the question of defining status within the kinship group, i.e. the definition of rights and obligations between a child and relatives other than parents. This is a cultural rather than a biological matter and involves the application of rules of descent. These again vary widely between societies but may be subsumed under two main headings. *Patrilineal descent* allocates the major rights and obligations regarding a child to the *father's* blood relatives (called consanguinal relatives by anthropologists). *Matrilineal descent* allocates these rights and obligations to the mother's consanguinal relatives. *Bilateral descent*, found in our own society, relates children to specified relatives on both sides of the family. Rules of descent are particularly important in the economic area through the transmission of property rights. The most rigid rules in this connection are found in the inheritance of land in non-industrial societies. Rules of descent are also important in the political sphere of societies where authority is traditionally based. Shakespeare's historical plays provide dramatic evidence on this point.

The *family* is a particular kind of kinship group defined by the fact that its members occupy a common household. The simplest type of family unit, the *nuclear family*, consists of a married couple and their children. Another type, also found in our own society, is the *extended family* which typically includes three generations in one household. In Britain this type has been found to retain a surprising degree of importance in traditional working-class areas.[1]

Because marital partners have to be sought outside the family, people become involved in two nuclear families; one is the *family of orientation* into which a person is born, the other is the *family of procreation* which is established through marriage. It is obviously impossible for both the male and the female to remain with their families of orientation after marriage so that the problem of residence arises. There are three basic solutions to the problem. The first is for the couple to reside in or near the groom's house-hold, this is the rule of *patrilocal residence*; the second is to reside in or near the bride's household, this being the rule of *matrilocal residence*; the third is where the couple are expected to set up their home independently of either family of orientation, this is called the rule of *neolocal residence*. In all cases the sanctions surrounding the rule may be strict and formal or else flexible and informal.

Much has been written about the diminution of functions performed by the family in modern society, by sociologists as well as by social commentators. Economic, welfare, educational and recreational functions have increasingly become the province of specialized agencies outside the family.[2] The one function which remains firmly within the family is the socialization of children into the basic values, beliefs and behaviours of the social system.

It should be noted that the family is only one of many agencies involved in socialization, this process continues throughout the lifetime of an individual as he undertakes roles in a variety of situations.[3] The significance of the family lies in the fact that it undertakes the initial task of transforming the "barbarian" infant into a social actor and creates a basic framework of attitudes, values, beliefs and habits which influences the future development

[1] See M. Young and P. Willmott, *Family and Kinship in East London*, London, Routledge & Kegan Paul, 1957.

[2] See, for example, R. Winch, *The Modern Family*, New York, Holt, Rinehart & Winston, 1952. For an alternative view see R. Fletcher, *The Family and Marriage*, Penguin Books, 1962.

[3] For a full discussion of the socialization process see Bredemeier and Stephenson, *op. cit.*, chaps. 3 and 4.

of the individual. In later life external agencies such as peer groups, schools, employers and so on undertake socialization into specific roles but their influence is mediated by personality factors developed within the family.

The study of the family as a socializing agency has taken at least two distinct directions, one concentrating on the actual content of cultural transmission from one generation to another, the other on the consequences of specified familial experiences for subsequent personality development. Both kinds of study are concerned with continuity between generations but in the former case it is reflected as a similarity in the content of beliefs and attitudes mediated largely through conscious indoctrination, whereas in the latter case continuity is seen as a chain of action and reaction between parents and the child. The former concentrates on cognitive, verbalized elements of personality, whereas the latter concentrates on emotional, subsconcious elements along the lines suggested by Freud and other psychoanalysts.[1]

The idea of cultural transmission is particularly useful in explaining the persistence of socio-cultural groups over long periods of time in the face of changing membership. Such persistence is evident not only in the continuity of societies as distinctive entities, but also within societies in the transmission of social class membership. There has been considerable research in Britain which relates differences between working class and middle class parents on attitudes towards education to differences in educational performance by their children.[2] The most impressive empirical documentations of cultural transmission have accumulated around the transmission of political loyalties and orientations,[3] and around occupational preferences.[4]

[1] See, for example, J. Whiting and I. Child, *Child Training and Personality: A Cross-Cultural Study*, Yale University Press, 1953.

[2] For example, J. Douglas, *The Home and the School*, London, MacGibbon & Kee, 1964.

[3] For example, H. Hyman, *Political Socialization*, Free Press, 1959.

[4] Occupational continuity between fathers and sons has been the particular concern of students of social mobility, e.g. D. Glass, ed., *Social Mobility in Britain*, Routledge & Kegan Paul, 1954; also N. Rogoff, *Recent Trends in Social Mobility*, Free Press, 1953.

Studies concerned with the familial context of personality development range from Freudian preoccupations with subconscious factors to social psychological studies of attitude formation. These overlap to some extent with research on cultural transmission but differ in that they emphasize unintended outcomes of family interaction rather than the actual content of attitudes and beliefs, i.e. they are studies of motivation rather than cultural continuity. An illustration of this approach is provided by a recent cross-cultural examination of family structure and achievement motivation, undertaken by Glen Elder.[1] One proposition supported by the extensive literature on the subject is that family structures characterized by parental dominance often produce a low achievement motivation in children through denying them the opportunity to develop confidence by independent problem solving. A similar effect is observed where the family is dominated by the wife. Another proposition is that high achievement motivation, reflected in high educational attainment relative to measured ability, is most prevalent among persons who report democratic relations with their parents and an egalitarian relationship between the mother and father. These and other propositions are supported by social survey data from the United States, Britain, West Germany, Italy and Mexico.[2]

[1] G. Elder, Family structure and educational attainment, *American Sociological Review* **30** (Feb. 1965), 81.

[2] Originally collected by G. Almond and S. Verba for their study of political behaviour published as *The Civic Culture*, Princeton, 1963.

# CHAPTER 5

# THE STRUCTURAL–FUNCTIONAL
# APPROACH TO SOCIAL ANALYSIS

RATHER than devote a chapter to classifying and summarizing the numerous "theories" of society which have been put forward we shall confine our attention to one theoretical approach, this being known as structural–functional analysis or functionalism. The justification for this choice is that functionalism in one form or another has been a major influence in the development of sociology as a scientific discipline and currently dominates sociological theory. One prominent scholar has gone so far as to argue that functional analysis *is* sociological analysis and not merely a special approach.[1] Before taking up this argument and some of the criticisms which it has aroused we shall give a brief account of the concepts and assumptions underlying functionalism.

In the work of early sociologists like Herbert Spencer, functionalism was introduced as an extension of the biologically oriented conception of society as an organism. Even when biological terms were used as analogies, however, there was always the danger of appearing to say that society *was* an organism. It was therefore a considerable step forward when Emile Durkheim built up a systematic model of society in purely sociological terms.[2] Durkheim's formulation was further refined by two British anthropologists, Radcliffe-Brown and Malinowski. We shall begin with a

[1] K. Davis, The myth of functional analysis as a special method in sociology and anthropology, *American Sociological Review* **24** (Dec. 1959), 752.

[2] Apart from his actual research quoted previously see *The Rules of Sociological Method*, Free Press, 1938.

brief review of their position, taking Radcliffe-Brown first because he was closer to the Durkheimian tradition.[1]

In his work a society is seen as a set of actions and interactions among human beings which form a structure of relationships. The continuity of a given structure is maintained by various processes of interaction which constitute the functioning of the structure. Particular structural arrangements such as ceremonies, institutions and organizations may be analysed in terms of the contribution they make to the maintenance of the whole social system. Radcliffe-Brown suggests the hypothesis that every social system is character-ized by *functional unity*, i.e. a condition whereby the various parts of a system are sufficiently well-integrated to avoid the generation of conflicts which cannot be resolved or regulated. An extension of this hypothesis is the proposition that functional unity is a state of equilibrium towards which social systems tend; internal or external disturbances to the system will produce reactions making for the re-establishment of equilibrium. In the extreme case of radical disturbance and readjustment, e.g. revolution, the type of structure may be changed but the system will survive with some degree of continuity. Radcliffe-Brown emphasizes that not every element in the life of a community has a function: there may be obsolete relics of the past or activities which are simply irrelevant to societal continuity. He also points out that the same social usage may have different functions in different social structures.

The strategy of research presented by Radcliffe-Brown is based upon the proposition that the functioning of structural elements can only be observed through their effects on the thoughts, feelings and actions of individuals. This point is important to remember in view of subsequent accusations that he ignored the individual and placed undue emphasis upon the total social system as some kind of independent entity.

Malinowski sought to extend Radcliffe-Brown's concept of functionalism by emphasizing the functional links between the various institutional sectors of society and by taking the biological

[1] The following summary of his ideas is taken from A. Radcliffe-Brown, *Structure and Function in Primitive Society*, London, Cohen & West, 1952.

needs and mental welfare of individuals as the focus of functional analysis, rather than the survival or maintenance of the social system as a whole. This approach is most clearly exemplified in his observations on magic and superstition in primitive societies.[1] Malinowski points out the close association between magic and practical activities, arguing that magic is used only where experience, reason and technical ability are inadequate to ensure success or to control the environment. This is particularly so where practical activities involve an element of danger and arouse anxiety in individuals. The function of magic is therefore to supplement knowledge in controlling the environment and thereby to alleviate anxiety; there is a rational and an emotional aspect of magic rituals corresponding to this dual function. In supporting his theory Malinowski points to the "crucial test" provided by observations on the Trobriand Islanders of the South Pacific. In the inner lagoon of the island fishing is done by the easy, reliable method of poisoning. On the shores of the open sea, however, it is done under dangerous conditions with no guarantee of success. Malinowski then points out that "in the lagoon fishing, where man can rely completely upon his knowledge and skill, magic does not exist, while in the open sea fishing, full of danger and uncertainty, there is extensive magic ritual to secure safety and good results".[2] It should be noted that whereas Radcliffe-Brown, and before him Durkheim, concentrated on the contributions of structural elements such as magic rituals to the whole social system, Malinowski's concern in this example is with the origin and persistence of the structural elements themselves. In other words there is a fundamental difference in the focus of explanation. The difference is important because there has been a tendency to assume that by describing the contributions of an element to the maintenance of the whole social system, the origin and persistence of the element itself is also explained. In fact this assumption is only valid under limited conditions to be discussed later. The main point is that the explanation of societal persistence is a theoretical problem distinct

[1] B. Malinowski, *Magic, Science and Religion*, Free Press, 1948.
[2] *Ibid.*, p. 14.

from that of explaining the existence or persistence of particular societal elements. By taking individual needs and perceptions of situations as the focus of analysis Malinowski is able to throw light upon the latter problem without touching upon the former.

Although Durkheim, Radcliffe-Brown and Malinowski got away from the use of biological analogies their formulations still reflect the "organismic" approach and present a model of society which is too well integrated in terms of modern societies (their research being largely confined to primitive communities). The final emancipation of functionalism from biological and anthropological traditions, together with its establishment as the dominant theoretical approach in sociology, was largely the work of the American sociologist Robert K. Merton. Without claiming to put forward a coherent theory, Merton undertook the task of codifying the concepts and problems inherent in functional analysis.[1]

Regarding the elements to which functions are imputed, Merton argues that they must be patterned and repetitive, e.g. roles, customs, norms and modes of behaviour. In examining such elements the sociologist must sooner or later take account of the motivations of individuals because socio-cultural elements are merely abstractions from human behaviour. When we talk of the family performing the function of socializing children, for example, we are using a form of conceptual shorthand which must ultimately be reduced to specific, observable behaviour in order to undertake empirical research. In common usage the term function is used loosely to include conscious purposes as well as the objective consequences of patterned elements. Merton stresses that only the latter should be termed functions in order to avoid confusion. The consequences of structural elements for the social system may be of several kinds, the following is a summary of Merton's typology:

1. Consequences which make for the adaptation or adjustment of the social system to external and internal demands; these being

[1] R. K. Merton, *Social Theory and Social Structure*, chap. 1, Free Press, 1957.

called *functions*. Within this category there is a distinction between those consequences which are recognized and intended by the individuals concerned, i.e. *manifest functions*, and those which are not intended or recognized, i.e. *latent functions*.

A good example of what is meant by a latent function is provided by Burton Clark's study of the role of junior colleges in the American educational system.[1] The ostensible purpose of the junior college is to give high-school graduates additional opportunities for further education. Clark points out that many students who go to junior college would like to transfer to a university or a four-year college but lack the necessary ability. One of the unintended consequences of the junior college is to protect the institutions of higher education from an increased pressure of admission by mediocre students. They are given a "cooling-off" period during which they may adjust their educational plans to a more realistic appraisal of their own capabilities. The alternative would be for teachers to go through the painful procedure of telling young people that they were not good enough. It should be noted that the successful performance of the "cooling-off" function by the junior colleges is conditional upon the function remaining latent. If students and parents became aware of it then there would be a turning away from the colleges.[2]

2. Consequences which lessen the adaptation or adjustment of the social system; these are called *dysfunctions* and may also be manifest or latent.

3. Consequences which are irrelevant to adaptation or adjustment and therefore empirically unimportant; these are simply called non-functional consequences.

As the consequences of any given structural element may be partly functional and partly dysfunctional the problem is raised in undertaking research of drawing up some kind of balance sheet. The problem is complicated by the fact that what is functional for

[1] B. Clark, The "cooling-off" function in higher education, *American Journal of Sociology*, 65 (May 1960), 569.
[2] For an elaboration of this point see L. Schneider, The category of ignorance in sociological theory, *American Sociological Review*, 27 (Aug. 1962), 492.

one individual or group may be dysfunctional for others within a social system. It is therefore necessary to specify clearly the range of units affected.

Although Merton deliberately avoids the idea that the conditions of the survival or successful adaptation of a social system can be specified, it has become an important part of structural-functional analysis. We have referred to the idea in previous chapters in talking of basic and recurring problems which all societies must deal with. In the literature these problems are variously termed functional requirements, functional requisities and functional exigencies. The most important figure in elaborating the functional requirements of a social system is Talcott Parsons.[1] According to Parsons there are four "functional exigencies" which must be met by a social system in order to survive as a coherent entity. These are goal-attainment; adaptation; integration; and pattern-maintenance. Around each one cluster activities, roles and institutions tending to specialize in a particular functional area. The role of the politician, for example, is made up of activities primarily oriented to directing social action towards certain goals. Once goals have been defined for the community the problem arises of establishing a supply of facilities or resources; this involves adaptive activities which may be generally categorized as the economy. In the pursuit of collective goals role-playing must be co-ordinated and organized in order to minimize conflict and maximize efficiency. Within the context of whole societies we may point to legal institutions as one set of roles concerned particularly with integration. Finally the social system must ensure the maintenance of the value system, institutionally the performance of the pattern-maintenance function is centred around socializing agencies such as the family and school.

Although the listing of functional requirements is useful as a descriptive device for talking about social systems and provides a framework for comparing the structures of various societies, its value in empirical research remains to be proved. One difficulty is

[1] See, for example, T. Parsons, R. Bales and E. Shils, *Working Papers in the Theory of Action*, Free Press, 1953.

that there are no clear rules to help the researcher in allocating a particular role or activity to a particular functional area. The abstract categories must be translated into operational terms in order to formulate testable hypotheses.

Having given some idea of the main concepts of functional analysis we shall now discuss some criticisms and reservations which have been expressed about it. These have taken two main directions, the first concentrating on the extent to which functionalism exhausts the possibilities of sociological analysis, the second concerned with the adequacy of the approach in analysing social change.

## FUNCTIONAL ANALYSIS AND SOCIOLOGICAL EXPLANATION

Recent discussions of the role of functional analysis in sociological explanation have centred around Kingsley Davis's contention that sociological analysis in research situations is by definition functional analysis.[1] His definition of functionalism is a very broad one and not confined to any of the particular formulations mentioned above. His argument is that functionalists only claim that the mere existence of a social system, whether it be a society, an organization or a small group, implies some kind of social order and that sociologists must study the way in which this order is maintained. Functionalism is not a special approach to the study of social systems, it is only the adoption of the sociological perspective. The term functionalism was useful in establishing sociology as a special discipline and in fighting evolutionary theories but it has now outlived its usefulness and should be dropped. Non-functional analysis is either reductionist, i.e. it explains social facts in terms of non-sociological factors as in psychological or economic explanations of social system, or it is non-theoretical and merely describes or manipulates data without attempting to explain it.

The claim that sociological analysis is nothing more than the explanation of social facts in terms of social systems has stimulated

[1] Davis, *op. cit.*

many sociologists to re-examine other possibilities. Ronald Dore[1] argues that an equally valid alternative to functional analysis is to induce causal laws from observed regularities in limited areas of social behaviour.[2] Instead of beginning with a theoretically defined social system the causal approach builds one up on a piecemeal basis. Dore carries the argument further by defending the assertion that the social system approach makes for difficulty in handling causal explanation; he does so by examining how a statement concerning the function of something can be translated into a statement of cause and effect.

The problem arises because of the temptation mentioned previously to explain the existence of a structural element in terms of its function in the social system, i.e. to say that the function served by $X$ is also a cause of $X$. Such a statement would be valid if it could be shown: (a) that actors within the system were aware of the function of $X$, and (b) that they were able to introduce or maintain $X$ by deliberate action. In this case the function could be introduced as a link in a causal chain of events. This condition applies in some functional analyses, particularly in societies where considerable intellectual energy is expended in analysing functions and bringing them to the notice of other people. Apart from the activities of social critics and political commentators this is clearly seen in cases where social scientists are employed as advisers to industrial and political decision-makers. The point is, however, that one cannot assume the existence of such knowledge.

Another valid line of argument for translating functional statements into causal statements is based upon the evolutionary notion of selective survival. The argument may perhaps be clarified by applying it to what has been called the Davis–Moore theory of stratification.[3] This states that an unequal distribution of rewards,

[1] R. Dore, Function and cause, *American Sociological Review*, **26** (Dec. 1961), 843.
[2] The distinction between functional and causal analysis was in fact clearly stated by Emile Durkheim over 60 years ago, see *The Rules of Sociological Method*, pp. 89–97.
[3] K. Davis and W. Moore, Some principles of stratification, *American Sociological Review*, **10** (Apr. 1945), 242.

making for stratification into status groups, is necessary for the successful functioning of societies characterized by a division of labour. Under the division of labour people perform set tasks on a regular basis; some of these tasks are more closely tied to societal requirements than others and must therefore be differentially rewarded in order to attract sufficient people capable of performing them. The possibility is admitted of short-run distortions, e.g. artificial limitations of opportunity or the persistence of prestige in roles whose importance has been diminished by social change. In the long run, however, it is argued that rewards are adjusted to functional utility. In this case any stratified structure of positions involving differential rewards can be explained in part by the functional requirements of the social system concerned.

The justification of the theory in terms of evolutionary survival would run as follows. Social structures characterized by a division of labour but *not* by unequal rewards have not been able to survive as ongoing systems and have been forced to develop a system of unequal rewards or else have imitated other more successful societies. As Dore remarks this is logically valid but empirically implausible. In any case the theory would only explain stratification as a general phenomena. It is of little help in explaining the characteristics of particular stratification systems.

Another important point made by Dore is that functional statements (e.g. the family functions to socialize children) are generalized summaries of causal relations between recurring events (e.g. parents cause children to obey rules of behaviour) which are in turn generalizations about specific events occurring between particular individuals (e.g. when John refused to say "please" his mother smacked him). Although functional analysis may be useful as a preliminary conceptual approach in handling complex data there must be a constant effort to break down functional summarization into causal explanations related to individual behaviour. One of the dangers of functionalism is that by talking about the functions of the family, the requirements of society and so on these concepts may appear to represent real entities rather than intellectual artifacts. The endowment of abstract concepts with the characteristics of living beings is called *reification*; it is an occupational hazard of the sociologist which must be guarded against. It should be noted, however, that there is one sense in which concepts have an objective reality, this is where human beings use them as reference points for behaviour in everyday language. In this case the terms become objects of study as well as tools of analysis.

To return to our main theme, Dore concludes his argument by noting some alternatives to functional analysis. The historical approach, for example, asks questions about the causes of the unique events leading to the establishment of a particular structural element. The "static" approach on the other hand seeks causal links between structural elements or between the regular events which constitute them. These are both valid alternatives to searching for the functional or dysfunctional consequences of a structural element for a social system.

The need to go beyond functionalism in order to explore social phenomena more fully has been made also by George Homans in a slightly rhetorical attack.[1] His main point is that functionalism has served a useful purpose in directing attention to important problems, particularly the interrelations between social institutions, but that it is now a positive hindrance to the further development of sociology. The failure has not been an empirical one, Homans points "to many valuable research contributions, but a failure as a theory". By making a strict distinction between sociological propositions about social systems and psychological propositions about individuals, functionalists find it difficult to explain *why* things are so instead of merely what they are. As explanation is the essential purpose of theory this indicates a basic weakness in the approach. The construction of descriptive categories is only a preliminary stage in the pursuit of explanatory propositions. Homans argues that functionalism cannot go beyond this stage because the concepts are too general to allow logical deductions of a testable kind. In order to explain why structural elements exist

[1] G. Homans, Bringing men back in, *American Sociological Review*, **29** (Dec. 1964), 809.

and persist the sociologist must turn to propositions about the behaviour of men rather than the functioning of social systems.

## FUNCTIONALISM AND SOCIAL CHANGE

The second line of attack on the structural–functional approach centres on its inability to account for conflict and change in social systems. Homans stresses this point in the article cited above and illustrates it by referring to one of the few attempts to apply functionalism to social change, a book by Neil Smelser on the industrial revolution in Britain.[1] The theoretical section is written exclusively in terms of Parsonian functionalism, i.e. a social system is described as a set of interrelated roles and positions, governed by the principle of equilibrium and characterized by four functional exigencies. In actually dealing with the data on change, however, Smelser is forced to devise his own seven step model of the process by which industrial differentiation and technological innovation occurred. This model is couched exclusively in social psychological terms. Thus certain men were excited about the possibility of making quick fortunes or dissatisfied with existing modes of production and were led to invent or adopt labour-saving machinery. In order to explain the origin and direction of change Smelser has to look at the motivations and purposes of the men who performed such roles as entrepreneur, inventor, weaver, spinner and so on.

The deficiencies of functionalism in this respect are discussed by Pierre van den Berghe in an article comparing it with the Marxian approach.[2] The Marxian model of society places conflict at the centre of theoretical concern rather than regarding it as a temporary deviation from a supposedly normal state of equilibrium. The dominant characteristic in the functionalist model is an inherent tendency towards stability. Dysfunctional

[1] N. Smelser, *Social Change in the Industrial Revolution*, University of Chicago, 1959.
[2] P. van den Berghe, Dialectic and functionalism, *American Sociological Review*, **28** (Oct. 1963), 695.

threats to stability are either "institutionalized" or resolve themselves. Such change as occurs is typically gradual and functional; dramatic change tends to be confined to the periphery of the social structure and rarely affects the central elements. According to functional theory change may come from three main sources:

1. Adjustment to external disturbances such as a recession in world trade.
2. Structural differentiation in response to problems within the system, e.g. electoral reforms in response to political unrest.
3. Creative innovations within the system, e.g. scientific discoveries or technological advances.

The basic factor making for a normal condition of stability is an assumed consensus on values and collective aims which holds together the social system. Van den Berghe argues that while this assumption may hold for simple societies it cannot be applied automatically to complex, culturally pluralistic societies. In fact there are other bases for social cohesion such as economic self-interest and political coercion which permit stability even in the face of considerable dissension about values and goals. The main point, however, is that there is no theoretical or empirical justification for making conflict and dissension secondary to stability and consensus as characteristics of social systems.

While the assumption of value consensus could be jettisoned without destroying the basic framework of functionalism, this cannot be said of the concept of *dynamic equilibrium*, which is inherent in the definition of a system. The term dynamic is important because a well-integrated system may undergo rapid change without showing stress or tension sufficient to threaten its functioning. The concept of dynamic equilibrium enables functionalists to deal with adjustive changes to internal problems, e.g. the development of bureaucracy to cope with the problems of large-scale administration, also with adjustive change to externally induced challenges, e.g. the absorption of migrant groups. There are, however, several facts which functional theory cannot account for; van den Berghe lists them as follows:

1. Some reactions to external challenges are far from adjustive, they are indeed very often destructive and dangerous to the system.
2. Social systems may go through long periods of progressive disintegration, ending perhaps in civil war and partition, without much sign of "built-in" mechanisms for adjustment coming into operation.
3. Change can be very sudden and deep-rooted; this has been demonstrated particularly in the developing nations of Asia, Africa, and South America as well as in Russia and China.

Van den Berghe admits that there is probably a long-term tendency towards integration but in order to account for the facts listed above the equilibrium model must be modified. The direction which such modification should take is indicated by considering the conflict model of society. The major propositions are that change is ubiquitous and generated largely within the social system through conflict between opposing elements. The conflict occurs at various levels of analysis. At the level of ideas and values (as conflict between opposing scientific theories, ideological positions or policy proposals); at the level of conscious group interests (as social class conflict or political party rivalry); and at the level of inherent structural contradictions (an example is where trade union officials become estranged from rank-and-file members through participating in collective bargaining and attempting to see the employers' point of view). The main weakness of existing conflict models is that they tend to *assume* a polarization of opposites as an inherent tendency rather than as one of several possibilities.

Van den Berghe suggests two points of convergence between functionalist theory and conflict theory (remembering that theory is being used in the loosest possible way). Firstly, conflict and consensus can have opposite effects from those stressed in the respective approaches. As Lewis Coser has pointed out, conflict can have positive, integrative consequences for a system;[1] on the

[1] L. Coser, *The Functions of Social Conflict*, Free Press, 1956.

other hand consensus may harden into complacency, fanaticism or inertia and threaten the dynamic equilibrium of a system. Secondly, both approaches contain the idea of the restoration of equilibrium following a disturbance. In functionalism this appears as a continuous series of *ad hoc* adjustments whereas in the dialectical sequence of conflict models there is a recurring and inevitable cycle of equilibrium and disequilibrium.

Although it is useful to indicate such convergences as those described by van den Berghe, it is questionable whether any "theoretical synthesis" is possible or even desirable. It could well be argued that the two approaches deal to some extent with separate problems and that two theoretical approaches are therefore demanded. The conflict model is concerned basically with the explanation of historical change and in predicting its direction, this is quite separate from the problem of explaining the maintenance of social integration in the face of change.

Having given examples of the criticisms which have been made of functionalism in explaining social change it is only fair to give some of the arguments made in defence. There is, for example, Wilbert Moore's argument that social systems face basic problems to which no lasting solutions can be found; consequently change is an implicit characteristic of all systems rather than a special problem to be explained in non-structural terms.[1] Among the basic problems are inevitable uncertainties in socializing individuals, the scarcity of resources relative to human wants and inherent contradictions based upon the fact that individuals and collectivities in pursuing certain goals have to give up others. This line of argument has been accepted by critics as theoretically plausible but too general to explain specific changes in historical situations.

Shmuel Eisenstadt, in a recent article,[2] argues that these objections can be partly answered by recognizing that the general potentialities for change described by Moore, are transformed

---

[1] W. Moore, A reconsideration of theories of social change, *American Sociological Review*, **25** (Dec. 1960), 810.

[2] S. Eisenstadt, Institutionalization and change, *Am. Soc. Rev.* **29** (Apr. 1964), 235.

into historical realities through the process of institutionalization. This he defines as "the organization of a societally prescribed system of differentiated behaviour oriented to the solution of certain problems inherent in a major area of social life". The creation of institutional arrangements involves the definition of norms to ensure desired behaviour, criteria upon which to base decisions about the allocation of resources, and sanctions to uphold the normative structure. Eisenstadt's point is that this process of creation, definition and control in itself generates possibilities for change which can be specified in historical situations through undertaking a structural analysis of the system. He illustrates the point by drawing on his own extensive research into "centralized bureaucratic empires"; these include the Roman, Byzantine, Ottoman and Chinese Empires among others.[1]

This historical preview of the common structural elements found in these empires includes the following points:

1. The Empires were typically established on the initiative of rulers, drawn mainly from established aristocratic, tribal or feudal families.
2. Their common aim was to restore law in conditions of turmoil and establish a more centralized political system under their own control so that they might direct things independently of traditional authorities.
3. In external affairs the rulers placed great emphasis on military and expansionist goals.
4. In order to oppose traditional authority the rulers sought allies within the social system; these were mainly from (a) the predominantly urban-based economic and professional groups whose interests were opposed to the traditional ruling groups, and (b) the peasants or power urban strata who might be led to expect benefits from a change of political organization.

The extent to which the empire-builders succeeded in establishing centralized political control depended upon several specifiable

[1] See S. Eisenstadt, *The Political Systems of Empires*, Free Press, 1963.

social conditions. The main one was the existence of a large number of persons and resources free from traditional commitments such as kinship or feudal obligations, and consequently available for mobilization by the rulers. In initiating the process of institutionalization the rulers had to devise policies calculated to free or create resources for their own use, e.g. the establishment of an independent small-holding peasantry protected from feudal landlords. The pursuit of such policies, involving the discriminatory treatment of potential allies and enemies, created internal tensions and contradictions. For example, at the same time that the rulers were trying to limit the power of the aristocracy they were forced to rely upon established, traditional symbols of status in allocating rewards. The conferring of a title would be useless as an inducement to loyalty if traditional values were completely changed. Another inherent contradiction was that the bureaucracies created as instruments of power tended to develop their own political goals and activities in ways which threatened the power of the rulers. In some cases officials used their power to acquire the traditional symbols of status and merely replaced those in traditional authority. In other cases they tried to make their own official positions hereditary through nepotism and thus threatened the efficiency of the bureaucracy. At the other extreme officials were kept under such close control that they lacked sufficient authority to perform their administrative tasks properly. The main conclusion of Eisenstadt's study is that the process of institutionalizing the political goals and organizations of the Empires created similar problems and a specifiable range of potential solutions. The direction and intensity of change can therefore be analysed in terms of the particular structure undergoing change and the solutions adopted to the problems of institutionalization.

Although Eisenstadt demonstrates that generalizations concerning historical change can be translated into the vocabulary of structural functional analysis, and that the translation is helpful in making comparative studies, there is little to indicate that the concepts and propositions of structural–functional theory are of much help in actually explaining the dynamics of change. It is noticeable that Eisenstadt's own explanations, as distinct from his descriptions, are couched in social psychological terms. For example the main sources of change in the Empires studied are described in the following terms (the emphases are our own):

1. "the continuous *needs* of the rulers for different types of resources and especially their great *dependence* on 'flexible' resources;"
2. "the rulers' *attempts* to maintain their own positions of control of both traditional legitimation and effective political control over the more flexible forces."
3. "the development of various autonomous *orientations* and *goals* among the major strata."

The article tends to support Homans's contention that the demands of empirical explanation force even confirmed structural-functionalists to rely on social psychological concepts.


## CONCLUSION

While it may be agreed that functional theory has failed in its lack of explanatory power, it is recognized that it has sensitized sociologists to a wide range of empirical problems, produced some impressive research, and provided a convenient conceptual framework for discussing and describing social data. Moreover the empirical success of functionalism has provided many "facts" to be explained, particularly the interrelations of structural elements, which could not have been arrived at by starting with the "piecemeal" approach advocated by Dore. There is also the point that social psychological factors such as goals, attitudes and values are created and manifested within a social structural context so that it is necessary to have some means of analysing this context before we can indulge in social psychological explanation. The structural–functional approach provides one such means of analysis.

Finally, it may be noted that although functionalism was

developed and has been discussed here, as an approach to the study of whole societies, it has achieved its greatest successes when applied to more limited social systems such as prisons, hospitals and business organizations. In these cases the system of roles is clearly defined and it is possible to reduce the general concept of the adaptation of a system to quantitative indices of efficiency or morale.[1] These provide precise criteria for deciding whether a given structural element or arrangement is functional or dysfunctional, a task which presents tremendous difficulties in studying whole societies. Whereas limited social systems often have specific goals, societies have very diffuse aims whose achievement or non-achievement is difficult to assess. In this case the classification of consequences as functional or dysfunctional becomes a matter of informed judgement and arguable plausibility rather than empirical demonstration.

[1] As an example of functional analysis within a limited system of interaction the reader may consult P. Blau, *The Dynamics of Bureaucracy*, University of Chicago, 1955.

# CHAPTER 6

# MIDDLE-RANGE THEORIES OF
# SOCIAL BEHAVIOUR

IN THE midst of debates about the possibility of a science of society and the feasibility of universally valid generalizations in sociology, there is a continuing growth of research in numerous limited spheres of investigation. In many of these spheres there has accumulated a coherent body of facts, concepts and generalizations which correspond to what Robert Merton has called "theories of the middle-range". Merton defines these as "theories intermediate to the minor working hypotheses evolved in abundance during the day-by-day routines of research, and the all-inclusive speculations comprising a master conceptual scheme from which it is hoped to derive a very large number of empirically observed uniformities of social behaviour."[1] The conceptual formulations which we shall consider in this chapter are of this nature. They are not theories in the rigorous sense as defined in our first chapter, but are sufficiently well developed to draw together a wide range of facts and to generate testable propositions. We shall call them theories as a matter of convenience and common sociological usage. Our discussion is presented under two headings; the first being reference group theory, the second, theories of deviant behaviour.

## REFERENCE GROUP THEORY

Mustafa Sherif, in an early formulation, defined reference groups as "those groups to which the individual relates himself as a

[1] R. K. Merton, *Social Theory and Social Structure*, 2nd ed., Introduction, Free Press, 1957.

part or to which he aspires to relate himself psychologically".[1] The definition points clearly to the importance of defining the groups with which an individual identifies, whether or not he belongs to them. This is necessary for a clearer understanding of his attitudes, values and aspirations, particularly changes which occur in them as he goes from one situation to another and different reference groups become salient for him. In our first chapter we discussed the process of "embourgeoisement" and noted that it included a shift in the identification of lower status persons from traditional working class groups to middle class groups. The outward signs of this change of identification are various but might include changes in speech, in political attitudes, in style of dress or in recreational pursuits.

From an empirical viewpoint it is important to remember that the individual is exposed directly or indirectly (through reading, conversation or the mass media) to diverse and sometimes contradictory models of social behaviour. These coexist in the mind of an individual at any given time so that the problem is not merely that of discovering which groups he identifies with but to which ones he gives priority in particular situations. The difficulties of investigation are increased by the fact that an individual often uses reference groups which are far removed from his own sphere of interaction. They may even be constructions of his own or another's imagination. Advertising is rich in examples of the creation of artificial reference groups for the manipulation of consumer behaviour.

An important distinction, both theoretically and empirically, is that between reference group and membership group. Quite often an individual is torn between the demands of a membership group with which he does not identify and the motivational dictates of a reference group of which he is not a member. This is one instance of what social psychologists call *marginality*. A familiar example is that of the foreman who is officially a member of the management group but who identifies with the workers on the shop-floor.

[1] M. Sherif, *Group Relations at the Crossroads*, New York, Harper, 1953.

E

As an example of the research on reference groups as a source of attitudes and standards of behaviour (i.e. as *normative* reference points), we shall discuss Theodore Newcomb's classic study of students at Bennington Women's College in the United States.[1]

One of the empirical findings which Newcomb sought to explain was a clear contrast between the political conservatism of first year students and the non-conservatism of older ones. In order to make sure that the difference was not due to changes in the political climate outside the college, Newcomb made repeated observations over a four year period. He was able to show that there was a shift in individual attitudes from conservatism to non-conservatism as the students progressed through the college. As examples of the contrast we may note that a mock election in 1936 showed 62 per cent of the first year students voting Republican, whereas only 14 per cent of third and fourth year students did so. Similarly only 9 per cent of the first year voted socialist or communist, whereas 30 per cent of the third and fourth year did so. In each of the four years of observation these differences were repeated, not only in voting figures but on measurement scales covering nine different issues related to conservatism and non-conservatism.

Another finding of significance was the considerable prestige attached to non-conservatism; this was seen in the voting results for the most worthy students to represent the college in hypothetical situations. The finding held for first year students as well as others and indicates one of the motivational factors making for a change of attitude. The informal social pressures within the college making for non-conservatism contrasted with the predominantly conservative orientations encouraged in the students' home lives. For most of them the college and the family constituted conflicting reference groups in political matters. The students showed a general awareness of the conflict and were also aware of the relationship between their own attitudes and those of senior, high prestige students. The awareness factor is important because

[1] Described in T. Newcomb, *Social Psychology*, New York, Dryden, 1953.

without it there would be no grounds for explaining the findings in terms of reference group theory.

Newcomb selected the most conservative and least conservative *senior* students for intensive interviewing in each of the four years of the research period and was able to make several generalizations regarding the differences between them. As we are concerned with illustrating the application of reference group theory, only those aware of their political position relative to that encouraged in the college community are considered here.

Conservative senior students used the college community as a *negative* reference group regarding politics and the family as a *positive* one. By maintaining their identification with the family reference group they were able to resist membership group pressures to change their attitudes. Within the conservative category, however, there was a distinction between those who had used the college community as a *general* negative reference group and those who used it as such *only* in the limited sphere of politics. Both types tended to be of low prestige in the college but the former were also regarded as being anti-social by other students.

The non-conservatives were also divided into those perceived as anti-social and those perceived as generally identifying with the college community. The former tended to be oriented towards academic rather than social pursuits and used the members of staff or academically outstanding students as positive reference groups of a general kind. They tended to use the college community generally as a negative reference group *except* within the sphere of politics. The latter were of high prestige, being formal or informal leaders of the community, and used the college generally as a positive reference group in political and other matters. Many of them also used their families as negative reference groups.

We have only been able to indicate some of the findings in Newcomb's study but they illustrate the usefulness of reference group theory in accounting for attitude change as well as the way in which a person may use a reference group to maintain non-conformist attitudes in the face of pressures from the immediate membership group.

The conceptual elaboration of reference group theory has been greatly stimulated by Robert Merton and Alice Kitt's paper[1] on the famous "American Soldier" studies.[2]

The authors begin by noting that Stouffer and his colleagues found contradictions between the demands made on the enlisted men by the official norms of the Army and the demands made upon them by the unofficial norms of their primary membership groups. In the language of reference group theory conformity to the non-membership group norms of officers involved non-conformity to primary membership group norms. From the viewpoint of functional theory the question arises as to the functions or dysfunctions of conformity to non-membership groups. The answers to this question must be considered in terms of the consequences of such conformity, (a) for the individual, (b) for his membership group, and (c) for the whole social system, in this case the Army.

For the individual there are two main functions arising from identification with a non-membership group (i.e. from what the authors call *anticipatory socialization*). The first is to make it easier for him to gain entry into the non-membership group, the second is to make adjustment easier after entry. In the study being considered, the first function was illustrated by the fact that those privates who identified with the official norms were more likely to get promotion. The second was not directly investigated in the study but could be tested as a hypothesis by comparing the adjustment of promoted men differing in degree of anticipatory socialization.

In so far as the benefits of anticipatory socialization depend on gaining access to the desired group it follows that denial of access will have dysfunctional consequences for the individual. The most important of these are status frustration and loss of acceptance in his membership group. This is the classic dilemma of the "marginal

[1] R. Merton and A. Kitt, Contributions to the theory of reference group behaviour in R. Merton and P. Lazarsfeld, eds., *Continuities in Social Research: Studies in the Scope and Method of "The American Soldier"*, Free Press, 1950.

[2] S. Stouffer *et al.*, *The American Soldier* (2 vols.), Princeton University Press, 1949.

man" who seeks to join a reference group from which he is excluded, and in doing so is rejected by the group to which he already belongs. One of the factors determining the probability of anticipatory socialization having functional or dysfunctional consequences for the individual is the extent to which the social structure provides avenues of mobility from one group to another. This is particularly important in analysing social class mobility. Although identification with a non-membership group may be functional for the individual it is frequently dysfunctional for his membership group in that it threatens internal cohesion and solidarity. The recognition of the threat by group members explains much of the hostility directed at out-group identifiers, reflected in such terms as traitor, snob, "crawler" and "blackleg".

From the viewpoint of the whole social system, in this case the Army, it might appear that anticipatory socialization is purely functional because it supports the official norms. The authors point out, however, than if it causes primary groups to disintegrate then morale could be adversely affected and the efficiency of the Army as a fighting force diminished.

Further implications are drawn out by considering the social processes which encourage or discourage identification with a non-membership group. Transferences of identification viewed with such hostility by group members may be studied more objectively as processes of social mobility or the cultural assimilation of minority groups. One factor encouraging the appearance of out-group identifiers is a deterioration of social relations within a group so that many members feel alienated from it. At the level of whole societies there may be such a deterioration in the rewards men experience as law-abiding members of society that they are motivated to transfer their loyalty to other societies and become traitors or else to some imagined future society, as in the case of Communist revolutionaries.

So far we have concentrated on the function of reference groups in providing norms of thinking, feeling and behaving, hence the use of the term normative function. It has been pointed out, however, by several students that they also perform an *evaluative function*.[1] The extent to which an individual feels satisfied with the various rewards and experiences which derive from his participation in society depends not merely upon the objective nature of his experiences, but upon the criteria which he uses to evaluate them. These criteria include the perceptions an individual has of the rewards and conditions of others. It is apparent that evaluative or comparative reference points may be individuals as well as groups so that this extension of reference group theory involves a more general terminology and a broader range of empirical referents.

In the Merton and Kitt article referred to above there is a short section on the use of reference groups as evaluative criteria, but they do not distinguish this from the normative function in a systematic way. The section occurs in discussing the enlisted men's evaluations of the fairness of the call-up system. The soldiers themselves often raised the question of the fairness of this and other institutional arrangements such as the promotion system, without prompting from the interviewers. Imputations of unfairness or injustice depended partly on who an individual compared himself with. Older married men were more likely than younger married men to think it unfair that they were called up, because of the large number of civilians in this category who had been exempted. Dissatisfaction of this kind has been termed *relative deprivation*.

Martin Patchen has attempted an experimental verification of some hypotheses suggested by the concept of relative deprivation;[2] the results are not of much sociological interest in themselves but an account of the experiment will help clarify the concept as well as illustrating the process of scientific verification, discussed in our opening chapter.

Patchen begins by distinguishing two types of satisfaction influenced by reference group standards:

1. Satisfaction derived directly from the performance of activities or the consumption of rewards.

---

[1] For example, H. Kelley, Two functions of reference groups, in E. Swanson *et al.*, eds., *Readings in Social Psychology*, New York, Henry Holt, 1952.

[2] M. Patchen, The effect of reference group standards on job satisfactions, *Human Relations*, 11 (4) (1958), 303.

2. Satisfaction with the norms governing the allocation of activities or rewards.

The author cites other studies indicating that the second type, related to feelings of justice or injustice, affects the first type, involving the enjoyment of what one has. On the basis of the existing literature Patchen puts forward two specific hypotheses for testing:

1. Persons experiencing a relative advantage in comparison with others doing the same job will enjoy it more than those experiencing a relative disadvantage (i.e. relative deprivation).
2. Persons experiencing a relative advantage will be more satisfied with the rules governing the allocation of work than those experiencing a relative disadvantage, even though both are doing the same work.

The subjects for the experiment were American high school pupils aged 13–14. The general design of the experiment was to compare the satisfactions expressed by three groups of subjects; each group performed a task (copying a list of numbers) which was known from previous questionnaire responses to be of moderate attraction to each person. The groups differed, however, in the reference points available for comparison; one group was made to feel relatively advantaged, another relatively disadvantaged, and the third (the control group) had no salient reference point.

In the advantaged situation the experimental group copied numbers while their classmates performed the extremely unpopular task of putting 100 names in alphabetical order. In the "relatively deprived" situation the experimental group copied numbers but their classmates performed the very popular task of modelling clay. In the non-comparison situation the control group copied numbers and so did their classmates.

Obviously in comparing the groups it was desirable that the members of them should be as similar as possible so that any difference in satisfaction could be attributed only to differences in the reference group situation. The members of the experimental groups were therefore matched on liking for the copying task (expressed on a seven-point scale); on liking for the task that their classmates were doing; and intelligence scores. It was also ensured that the sex distribution within the groups was the same as that in the class generally, and that at least one of each group member's friends was outside his job group. These two operations were designed to maximize the probability that the rest of the class would in fact be perceived as a reference point.

The assessment of rules satisfaction included questions on the fairness of procedures for allocating jobs, the adequacy of the instructions they were given and of the time allotted for the completion of work. There were also direct questions on enjoyment and interest.

The data supported the hypothesis concerning job enjoyment in that both the advantaged and the control groups showed a statistically significant higher degree of enjoyment than the deprived group. There was, however, no support for the hypothesis concerning rules satisfaction. In fact the advantaged group complained rather more than either of the other two which was a reversal of the predicted direction. These two findings were confirmed by looking at the relationship between the reference group situation and satisfaction for all subjects, i.e. for the classmates as well as the experimental groups. There was a high relationship with job enjoyment but a negligible one with rules satisfaction. There were, in fact, two other factors independently and highly related to rules satisfaction; they were submissiveness to authority (measured by a standardized attitude scale) and sex (females showing higher rules satisfaction). Neither factor had been included in the orginal hypotheses, however. Patchen further notes that job enjoyment had no effect on the amount or quality of work done.

In the interpretation of his findings concerning rules satisfaction Patchen suggests that a reference group may provide a criterion for what may be *realistically hoped for* and thus influence the enjoyment of a job, without providing a criterion for what a person feels *entitled to*. The problem is, therefore, to determine the conditions under which reference groups are used as normative standards as well as realistic hopes. Certainly such factors as the intensity of relative deprivation, the prospect of its continuation and the importance for the individual of what is being experienced would have to be considered. We would also add that normative standards are created as part of a group culture and that they would be unlikely to appear in the kind of temporary, "artificial" situation set up for experimental purposes.

The application of reference group theory to job satisfaction has also been made in "real-life" situations; an article by William Form and James Geschwender provides a good illustration.[1] Their general proposition is that "personal evaluations of life situations are relative to the precise social locations which people occupy in society and the specific groups to which they commit their identities". The research undertaken by Form and Geschwender concentrates on the job satisfaction expressed by manual workers in an American city. Existing studies of manual workers indicate that they do not believe in personal opportunities for gaining promotion in an occupational hierarchy. In fact, many of them have no clear conception that such a hierarchy, translated into a more general social status hierarchy, exists. Lacking the awareness and motivation for social climbing which characterizes the middle classes, they tend to evaluate their jobs in terms of immediate rewards rather than in terms of achieved or anticipated social mobility. If this argument is valid then instead of following the middle class pattern of using hierarchal status groups as reference points, they will use workmates and relevant family members. It is further argued that lacking the expectation of social mobility they will not experience dissatisfaction from the mere fact of immobility. In other words the notion of status frustration is held to be largely irrelevant to the working classes. The explanation for this is given in terms of anticipatory socialization during childhood (i.e. identification with working class

---

[1] W. Form and J. Geschwender, Social reference basis of job satisfaction: the case of manual workers, *American Sociological Review*, 27 (Apr. 1962), 228.

F

persons and groups), and the adaptation of aspirations to perceived opportunities after entering work.

The specific hypotheses derived from the above propositions were as follows:

1. The relation between actual status level and parental aspirations for the manual worker will have no effect on job satisfaction. For example, if a worker's parents wanted him to be a doctor and he became a factory hand this would not in itself produce job dissatisfaction.
2. There will be a positive association between job satisfaction and the occupational status of the manual worker relative to that of his father.
3. The same relationship will hold for occupational status relative to that of his brother (only those having one working brother were considered).
4. Job satisfaction will be positively associated with occupational status relative to that achieved by persons of similar social background (indicated by similarity in father's occupation).

The sample of 545 respondents was made up of 11.4 per cent unskilled workers; 26.8 per cent skilled workers; 59.8 per cent semi-skilled workers; and 2 per cent "manual clerical", i.e. low grade clerical workers.

The first hypothesis could not be tested because only 77 respondents reported that their parents had any aspirations for them, this being insufficient for statistical analysis. The second hypothesis was confirmed in that those having a higher occupational status than their fathers showed significantly higher job satisfaction scores than those whose status was lower. The fact that those on the same level as their fathers showed nearly as much satisfaction as those on a higher one indicates that immobility is as satisfactory as limited upward mobility for the manual worker. One would not expect this to be so amongst middle-class persons.

The third hypothesis was also confirmed, and in this case the satisfaction of those with a higher status than their brothers was significantly higher than those on the same level. The fourth hypothesis was supported by the data and indicates that friends and peers are salient reference points in evaluating job satisfaction.

In discussing their findings the authors suggest that the observed relationships between satisfaction and immediate social reference points will hold as long as the manual worker does not accept the middle-class ideology of the possibility and desirability of upward social mobility. If he does accept it then the reference points will tend to shift from peers, parents and relatives to abstract status groups or to the incumbents of positions perceived as superior to his own. In this case he will experience a blocking of aspiration and a consequent dissatisfaction with his occupational level. The social significance of such dissatisfaction rests upon the frequently observed fact that the barrier between manual and white-collar occupations is very difficult to surmount. If educational or other socializing agencies succeeded in spreading middle-class ideology to lower status groups then a significant increase in frustration and dissatisfaction would be expected. This in turn could be of such intensity as to induce a normative dissatisfaction with the rules of society. Such phenomena as radical reform movements, political apathy or Negro rioting in the United States could well be illuminated by reference group theory.

As a final example of the empirical application of the theory we turn to an article by Lipset and Trow on collective bargaining.[1] This also serves to illustrate the function of middle-range theories in encouraging interdisciplinary research.

The authors begin by noting the inadequacy of orthodox economic theory in accounting for the behaviour of trade unionists and management in collective bargaining. The inadequacy has been recognized by labour economists themselves and increasing attention is being paid to non-economic factors. Only by looking at subjective factors such as feelings of injustice or standards of fairness can we explain such phenomena as economically absurd and self-defeating strikes, why the size of the wage adjustment is

---

[1] S. Lipset and M. Trow, Reference group theory and trade union policy, in M. Kamarovsky, ed., *Frontiers of the Social Sciences*, p. 391, Free Press, 1957.

often more important than the absolute size of the wage packet for union negotiators, and why unions insist on multi-union and multi-employer bargaining structures when they could get more by negotiating separately with each employer.

The labour economist is forced to make assumptions about the criteria used by negotiators in collective bargaining. Lipset and Trow contend that their analyses would be improved if this were done in the light of theoretical and empirical knowledge accumulated in the other social sciences rather than on an *ad hoc* basis. As a first step in the application of reference group theory to this field, a discussion is made of the main factors determining what kind of reference groups will be salient for the workers' representatives. They are grouped under four headings:

1. The socio-economic structure may pattern common frames of reference for persons in a given occupational category. It has been suggested, for example, that where occupational categories are under the same managerial authority due to large-scale, multiple ownership of employing units, they are likely to use each other as reference groups. It has also been suggested that workers in large unions are likely to use abstract reference points such as "steel workers" or "the working class", whereas those in small unions or small employment units are more likely to use specific, personal reference points such as workmates or neighbours.

2. Reference points may be created or made salient by institutional definitions. There are, for example, standards of fair comparison laid down by arbitration tribunals. These may not correspond to traditional standards accepted by the workers.

3. The choice and the emotional significance of reference points is influenced by norms and values in the overall cultural system. Some wage differentials such as those between skilled and semi-skilled workers or manual and white-collar workers are imbued with strong cultural sentiments which may cut across considerations of economic rationality. In this case one can see clearly the importance of negative reference groups.

4. Conflicts within or between the organizations of workers, employers and government may focus the appeals of leaders on to

particular reference groups as a matter of political strategy. Studies of collective bargaining reveal deliberate attempts to manipulate the reference groups of workers in order to gain particular ends. It is suggested that under conditions of conflict, either within unions or between them and other organizations, there will be a greater appeal to abstract reference groups due to their usefulness for propaganda purposes. The likelihood is all the greater where conflict is conducted openly and public opinion is involved.

As a conclusion to this section we should emphasize that more space has been devoted to reference group theory than is strictly merited by its importance in contemporary sociology. The justifications for this are (a) that the ideas are simple to grasp yet far-reaching in their implications and, therefore, ideal for an introductory textbook; (b) propositions concerning relative deprivation, anticipatory socialization and so on have an explanatory value which is rare in sociology; (c) the ideas are readily amenable to research over a wide range of social phenomena and thereby stimulate comparative and interdisciplinary thinking.

## THEORIES OF DEVIANT BEHAVIOUR

The development of theoretical formulations concerning deviant behaviour, like reference group theory, owes much to the contributions of Robert K. Merton. We shall, therefore, begin with a summary of the main points of a seminal essay by him.[1] Not the least of its merits for purposes of our discussion is its consciously sociological orientation. This is clearly seen in the stated aim of discovering "how some social structures exert a definite pressure upon certain persons in the society to engage in nonconformist rather than conformist conduct". The general formulation of the problem is the same as that made by Emile Durkheim in studying suicide. Just as Durkheim was concerned with explaining variations in rates of suicide rather than individual suicides, so Merton is concerned with rates of deviant behaviour rather than the

[1] R. Merton, Social structure and anomie, in *Social Theory and Social Structure*.

individual deviant. Whatever the merits of psychological theories, e.g. the Freudian notion of man in conflict with "artificial" social restraints, they are in themselves inadequate to explain differential patterns of deviant behaviour between social groups or societies.

Merton's central proposition is that structural pressures towards deviance arise from discrepancies between culturally engendered goals, on the one hand, and the availability of legitimate means for attaining them on the other. *Cultural goals* refer to those rewards, objectives and ambitions which the individual is encouraged to regard as worthwhile ends through socialization. Complementary to these goals there are prescribed ways of pursuing them which Merton calls *institutionalized means*. Individuals must be motivated to accept both the goals and the means for the social system to function properly, therefore rewards must be derived from the actual process of pursuing goals as well as in attaining them. In societies where goals are highly stressed but which provide inadequate means or inadequate motivation to conform to the means, there is a danger that people will follow the most effective ways of getting what they want regardless of whether these are legitimate. If this situation is carried far enough then the social system reaches a condition of instability and "normlessness" which Durkheim termed *anomie*.[1] Merton argues that contemporary American society has almost reached such a condition because there has been an effective stress on goals such as monetary success and unlimited social climbing[2] without an adequate provision of legitimate avenues of achievement. His own definition of anomie, following Durkheim, is "a breakdown in the cultural structure, occurring particularly where there is an acute disjunction between cultural norms and goals and the socially structured capacities of members of the group to act in accord with them".

\part from providing a means of explaining the varying ـures exerted on persons through the social structure and their

[1] The reader may recall our discussion of anomic suicide in a previous chapter.

[2] The extent to which the stress has been effective in the socialization of lower status persons is questionable and weakens Merton's claim that American society as a whole is becoming more anomic.

position within it, Merton's formulation also provides the basis for a descriptive typology of deviant behaviour.[1] Given the two primary elements (i.e. cultural goals and institutionalized means) it is theoretically possible for an individual to accept or reject either of them. Also the rejection may be merely passive or it may involve the active substitution of non-legitimate means. In diagrammatic form the typology appears as follows:[2]

| Cultural goals | Institutional means | Type of deviance |
|:---:|:---:|:---|
| + | ± | Innovation |
| − | + | Ritualism |
| − | − | Retreatism |
| ± | ± | Rebellion |

N.B. + = acceptance; − = passive rejection; ± = rejection and substitution.

In terms of the typology a criminal is one who accepts the cultural goal of monetary success but adopts illegitimate means for pursuing it, he thereby indulges in "innovation". Other familiar social types such as the bohemian, the revolutionary and the eccentric can be similarly placed in various categories.

The importance of differential access to legitimate means of goal-attainment in explaining and predicting deviant behaviour has been qualified in subsequent elaborations of the theory undertaken by Richard Cloward.[3] He proposes that an equally important factor is *differential access to illegitimate means*, these being contradictory to generally accepted norms but not necessarily against the law. The point is that some individuals through their social backgrounds and spheres of interaction find it easier than others to learn and utilize illegitimate means; they have the

[1] See Merton, *op. cit.* (rev. ed.), chaps. 4 and 5.

[2] For a more satisfactory extension of the typology, based upon a distinction between institutional norms and actual behaviour, see R. Dubin, Deviant behaviour and social structure, *American Sociological Review*, **24** (Apr. 1959), 147.

[3] See R. Cloward, Illegitimate means, anomie, and deviant behaviour, *American Sociological Review*, **24** (Apr. 1959), 164; also R. Cloward and L. Ohlin, *Delinquency and Opportunity*, Free Press, 1960.

"know-how" and the contacts. Sutherland's study of the professional thief[1] illustrates the operation of such factors. The successful thief needs to have certain personal qualities, a professional training and be accepted by other thieves as a qualified member of the profession. The mere motivation to steal is, therefore, inadequate to account for this particular type of deviant behaviour. There are deviant sub-cultures, having a residential basis, which provide learning experiences and opportunity structures parallel to those provided in the legitimate areas of society. Access to illegitimate means may be further broken down into (a) differential exposure to illegitimate attitudes and norms during childhood, and (b) differential exposure to opportunities for practising illegitimate means in adult life.

The first element was the primary focus of a particular body of theory and research described by Cloward as the "cultural transmission" or "differential association" school. Its founders included Edwin Sutherland, Clifford Shaw and Henry McKay.[2] Much of their work consists of ecological and anthropological studies of lower-class neighbours in Chicago. They noted the concentration of delinquency in these areas and described the way in which criminal values were transmitted so as to perpetuate deviant sub-cultures even where socio-economic conditions improved. They also described the ways in which young people acquired the skills necessary for a successful career in crime and were then recruited into criminal organizations. The well-integrated deviant sub-culture of a criminal neighbourhood is an extreme case of access to illegitimate means.

By incorporating the cultural transmission approach into the theory of anomie, formulated by Merton, Cloward hoped to provide a coherent framework for the analysis of deviant behaviour. As an example of how the extension of the theory of anomie could be applied he attempts to specify the conditions under which the "retreatist" type of deviant behaviour arises.

[1] E. Sutherland, ed., *The Professional Thief*, University of Chicago, 1937.
[2] See C. Shaw *et al.*, *Delinquency Areas*, Chicago, 1940; C. Shaw and H. McKay, *Juvenile Delinquency and Urban Areas*, Chicago, 1942.

In Merton's typology this involves not only a rejection of cultural goals but also a withdrawal from attempts to attain them. It includes the behaviour of persons like the drug addict, the alcoholic and the tramp. Merton saw retreatism as arising in cases where there is a failure in the use of legitimate means of goal-attainment combined with internalized restraints concerning the use of illegitimate means. Cloward argues that retreatism may occur in the absence of such restraints of conscience, specifically through lack of access to illegitimate means or through lack of skills to make use of them. There are, therefore, at least two paths to retreatism apart from that proposed by Merton. It is suggested by Cloward that whereas middle- and upper-class retreatists are more likely to have taken the path described by Merton, due to the greater likelihood of having internalized restraints against illegitimate behaviour, those in the lower classes are more likely to have followed the path of failure in the use of both legitimate and illegitimate means. They are more likely to be failed "innovationists" than failed conformists.

A further revision of Merton's theoretical statements has appeared recently in an attempt by Albert Cohen,[1] famous for his work on delinquent gangs, to prepare the way for a general theory of deviant behaviour. Beginning with a critical review of Merton's original essay, he notes the following weaknesses:

1. Although the framework of his theory is sociological, dealing with cultural goals and institutionally patterned means, the actual process by which deviant behaviour arises is described in terms of "the individual", conceived as an abstract psychological entity rather than as a social actor. There is no reference made to the significance of the experiences a person may have of the stresses, failures, successes and modes of adaptation of *others*. The analysis of deviant behaviour requires an examination of the reference groups used for comparison and evaluation.[2] For example, a

[1] A. Cohen, The sociology of the deviant act, *American Sociological Review*, 30 (Feb. 1965), 5.
[2] Cohen recognizes Merton's own contribution to reference group theory but argues that he has not related it systematically to his theory of deviance.

person may have ready access to legitimate means of goal-attainment yet perceive others doing better than himself through illegitimate means. This could generate strains on conformity not allowed for in Merton's formulation; the schoolboy who sees others gaining high marks through cheating, the businessman who sees others prospering through sharp practices, and the young executive who watches promotion go to more ruthless and deceitful colleagues, are all faced with pressure making for deviance even though they themselves may be quite successful from an objective point of view.

2. Given the existence of a strain on conformity various solutions may be adopted, but here again the individual is affected by others. This factor is allowed for in Cloward's notion of illegitimate opportunity structures so that this gap in Merton's theory has been partially filled. Apart, however, from the existence of deviant sub-cultures which function as training grounds there is also the situation where a number of interacting individuals, subject to the same pressures on conformity, serve as reference points for each other and develop some kind of collective solution to their problems. The formation of delinquent gangs is one manifestation of this process.[1]

3. Merton's formulation treats the deviant act as though it were an abrupt change from conformity, whereas in real life it is more likely to be part of a gradual process of change characterized by "groping, advancing, backtracking and sounding-out". If deviant behaviour is seen as part of a process of interaction between the individual and others then it will in part be shaped by the responses he receives from them. In this case one must consider not only the structural pressures making for deviance but also the way in which deviant acts are responded to. Cohen suggests four major types of response:

(a) *Opening up legitimate opportunities.* This is sometimes done by specialized role-players, e.g. probation officers trying to

[1] See A. Cohen, *Delinquent Boys, The Culture of the Gang*, Free Press, 1955.

find suitable employment for delinquents, or it may be done as a matter of official policy, e.g. allowing addicts to obtain drugs by a doctor's prescription The general response is one of helping to cure or reform the deviant.

(b) *Closing legitimate opportunities.* This occurs where deviance results in being labelled and shut off from "respectable" society. The general response is one of ostracism and rejection.

(c) *Opening up illegitimate opportunities.* Instead of trying to control the deviant others may respond by co-operating with him, e.g. the doting mother who turns a blind eye to the behaviour of an erring son, or the "crooked" policeman who co-operates with criminals. This category also includes the more positive opening up of illegitimate opportunities provided by criminal organizations for promising recruits.

(d) *Closing illegitimate opportunities.* The clearest example of this type of response is the imprisonment of criminals but it includes all forms of restraint and surveillance.

A final point made by Cohen is that the notion of deviance as an adjustment to inadequate legitimate means or as an exploitation of illegitimate means does not explain all deviant behaviour. In some cases it is more plausibly explained as part of the acting out of a role, either as a kind of self-expressive symbolism or merely as an unanticipated consequence of entering a certain role. A young man may choose to become a jazz musician because he enjoys playing the piano but then find that the role includes elements of deviant behaviour which he must perform in order to be accepted. The self-conscious deviance of the "beatnik" on the other hand may be seen as an attempt to project a certain image of himself, to establish a certain identity, rather than as an adaptation to failure. In both cases the language of role theory[1] is better suited to explanation than the theory of anomie.

[1] The two major figures in developing the theory of role-playing as a means of self-identification are George Herbert Mead (see *Mind, Self and Society*, Chicago, 1934) and Erving Goffman (see *The Presentation of Self in Everyday Life*, New York, Doubleday–Anchor, 1959).

In fairness to Merton it should be remembered that his concern was to explain differences in rates of deviant behaviour between social groupings, rather than to explain individual acts of deviance. He emphasized one particular source of deviant behaviour because this was directly related to the social structure and to the different positions occupied by persons within it. The factors which Cohen examines as sources of deviant behaviour are relevant to Merton's problem only in so far as they in turn can be shown to be systematically related to position in the social structure, e.g. if it would be shown that responses to deviant acts vary according to the social status of the deviant. Certainly this kind of link-up is possible and we may agree with Cohen's conclusion that the social structural and social psychological approaches should be brought into a more rigorous theoretical alignment. Each approach can help explain the empirical problems of the other.

### THE EXPLANATION OF JUVENILE DELINQUENCY

We have so far concentrated on theoretical formulations concerning deviant behaviour generally. In this section we shall look at some empirical applications of these ideas in analysing one particular area of deviance, viz. juvenile delinquency. One or two difficult methodological problems will be touched upon but this is inevitable if we are to treat sociology as a science rather than a form of social description and comment.

According to Cloward's extension of the theory of anomie the prevalence of juvenile delinquency amongst given sections of the population depends upon the socially structured degree of access to legitimate means of goal-attainment *combined with* degree of access to illegitimate means. Both factors must be considered in conjunction. A major problem to be resolved before the theory can be applied is the way in which they combine to determine the probability of delinquency for persons occupying different positions in the social structure. As a preliminary statement we may say that while the restriction of legitimate opportunities generates psychological pressures towards delinquency, it is only useful as a predictor of the probability of delinquent behaviour when the availability of illegitimate means is also known.

The pressures generated by restricted opportunity constitute the dynamic element of the theory. It must be repeated that the theory only points to one of many possible motivations to disobey the law; it is emphasized because it is directly linked to position in the social structure and therefore helpful in explaining differential rates of delinquency. It is assumed that other kinds of motivation are empirically rare or that they are randomly distributed within the social system.

In so far as the combined effect of the two factors is theoretically posited as being greater than the effect of either factor considered separately, the probability of deviant behaviour is predicted not by adding them together but by multiplying, i.e. by their *product* not their sum. This may be made clearer by a hypothetical example using numbers.

Suppose that we have been able to measure the degree of restriction on access to legitimate means ($X$) and the degree of access to illegitimate means ($Y$) for several groups in the social structure; also that the values range from 0–10 on each factor. A high restriction score combined with a high success score would indicate a high probability of delinquency in a given group. Let us further assume that the scores for a particular group are $X = 8$ and $Y = 6$. If the factors were combined in an additive way the total score would be 14, whereas by combining them in a multiplicative way the total is 48, consequently a far higher level of delinquency is predicted. It may also be seen that a unit increase in one score would have a disproportional effect on the total score. The reasoning is that there exists a cumulative interaction between the factors. If it was empirically possible for the value of one factor to be zero, e.g. a complete lack of access to illegitimate means, then an absence of delinquency would be predicted.

Some light has been thrown on this aspect of Cloward's theory as well as on the more general problem of defining the structural factors most useful for predicting delinquency, in an article by

Erdman Palmore and Philip Hammond.[1] The authors selected for study every young person in an American metropolitan area who was (a) born between 1942 and 1944, and (b) whose supervising relative (usually the mother) was enrolled with the Aid to Dependent Children organization (ADC) in 1950. The 353 cases were investigated through their social casework records, school records and police records (where applicable); in each case the period covered was from the 6th to the 19th birthday. The group was fairly homogeneous in social background, all coming from homes which were economically deprived and disturbed by divorce, death or desertion. Given this background it is not surprising that the group as a whole showed a high delinquency rate; 34 per cent having been reported by the police as indulging in some kind of delinquency. The statistical data is analysed to determine which social characteristics, if any, distinguished the delinquent third from the others. Throughout the analysis the observed rates for various social categories are compared to the rates which would be expected if the theory of differential access to opportunity structures was correct. It should be noted that the data was not collected in order to test the theory, but is being used to assess the plausibility of its propositions.

Let us consider three findings related to the proposition that restricted access to legitimate means is related to the probability of delinquency.

1. Negroes had higher delinquency rates than white youths.
2. Boys had higher rates than girls.
3. Those failing to complete high school had higher rates than those succeeding.

Each of the three main factors associated with delinquency, race, sex and school performance, had an independent effect, i.e. the association with delinquency still held when the effects of the other two were allowed for. In terms of the theory it is argued that

[1] E. Palmore and P. Hammond, Interacting factors in juvenile delinquency, *American Sociological Review*, **29** (Dec. 1964), 848.

in the above findings the category with the higher rate of delinquency also has the lower access to legitimate opportunities. Negroes are known to be discriminated against in many spheres, particularly in obtaining or keeping jobs. Boys are more likely to experience barriers to opportunities than girls because their goals typically include occupational and financial goals, whereas girls can restrict themselves to more easily attained marital and familial goals. Boys are faced with more demanding criteria of success. Finally young people who drop out of school face greater difficulties than those who do not.

Each of these indicators of access to legitimate opportunities had not only an independent effect but also had a combined effect, the more barriers there were to opportunities the greater the probability of delinquency. The rate for Negro boys failing school was 71 per cent, while at the other extreme the rate for white girls succeeding in school was zero. Other combinations were intermediate and in expected order, e.g. white males failing school showed 61 per cent; white males succeeding in school showed 38 per cent; Negro females succeeding in school showed 24 per cent; white females failing in school showed 23 per cent.

The second major element in Cloward's theory concerns access to illegitimate opportunities. Palmore and Hammond found two factors with significant effects on delinquency rates which may be interpreted as indicators of this element. They were (a) *family deviance*, deviant families being classified as those characterized by a "gross deviation" such as one or both parents being in prison, multiple illegitimacies, or a series of illegitimate affairs by the parent; (b) *neighbourhood deviance*, deviant neighbourhoods being those having a relatively high delinquency rate.

The three major findings regarding the interaction effect of legitimate and illegitimate opportunity facters were

1. A deviant family background increased the probability of delinquency among Negroes but not among whites.
2. A deviant neighbourhood background increased the probability of delinquency among males but not females.

3. Either kind of deviant background increased the probability of delinquency among these failing school more than it did among those succeeding.

The main point is that exposure to illegitimate opportunities (assuming that the indicators had some validity) had a far greater effect on those with fewer legitimate opportunities. The authors give some figures suggesting that the observed rates correspond to the product rather than the sum of the two factors, but as the figures are used to illustrate rather than to test the theory we shall not give them here. Certainly there is sufficient evidence to demonstrate the influence of both factors and the necessity of considering them as interacting rather than independent variables. Further research is demanded, however, using more convincing indicators of access to legitimate and illegitimate means.

Empirical studies of juvenile delinquency and other kinds of deviant behaviour such as suicide or mental illness suggest that they occur most frequently amongst persons of low socio-economic status. It was in the context of such findings that the theories of Merton and Cloward were developed. Central to their approach is the idea that individuals are typically motivated to achieve a favourable self-image through attaining culturally defined success goals. Where goal-attainment is blocked by lack of access to legitimate means then the individual experiences frustration and resentment which predisposes him to seek or accept illegitimate means. This has been termed the "status frustration hypothesis". Its application to low status groups (roughly equivalent to the lower working class) involves several assumptions:

1. That low status persons are exposed to and accept the values and goals of society.
2. That they are frustrated in pursuing these goals by factors inherent in the social system.
3. The causes of their frustration are perceived by individuals as being located in the social system, i.e. low status persons typically have a clear perception of their own place in the

social structure and an accurate idea of their own and other people's chances of success.

A paper by Jack Roach and Orville Gursslin which examines the assumptions and questions their empirical validity, provides a useful focus for further discussion.[1] The assumptions listed above are contrasted with the following propositions based upon empirical research on lower status persons:

1. Lower status persons typically lack the motivation for educational and occupational achievement; this has in fact been put forward as a major factor in explaining the failure of educational and other reforms to overcome the disadvantage of a low status family background.

2. They have relatively unstructured and inaccurate perceptions of the social environment and little comprehension of alternative opportunities for self-advancement.

3. They do not think in terms of status approval by others on the middle-class pattern and show little evidence of experiencing frustration at their low status.

If these propositions are true there is little reason to accept the hypothesis of status frustration as an explanation of lower-class deviance, or the associated theory that it leads to the formation of deviant sub-cultures.

Having questioned the validity of status frustration explanations the authors present an alternative explanation based upon the fact of economic deprivation. Because of their condition of extended economic deprivation, lower status persons are confined to an impoverished socio-cultural sphere which induces intellectual retardation, poor verbal skills and an impaired capacity for undertaking varied role-playing. Consequently they find difficulty in coping with the demands of modern industrial society and the strain is manifested by signs of behavioural disorganization such as mental disorder, suicide and delinquency.

The importance of the above critique is not to suggest an *alternative* to the status frustration hypothesis, but to point out

[1] J. Roach and O. Gursslin, The lower class, status frustration and social disorganization, *Social Forces*, **43** (May 1965), 501.

that the hypothesis makes assumptions about motivations and perceptions which are probably invalid for important sections of the population. The same point could be made about other sociological propositions which assume a simplified, uniform model of the human personality. In fact, men have different "needs", different modes of perception, different kinds of motivation and different ways of ordering their lives; moreover these differences are systematically related to the social environment. This being so, it would appear dangerous to state sociological propositions as though they were universally valid to all societies or all sections of a single society. All of them assume something about individual behaviour and unless the assumptions are clearly specified the sociologist is in danger of imposing his own limited view of "human nature" upon his data. As this tends to be and educated, middle-class view it is not surprising that many sociological propositions require considerable modification when applied to other social groupings, particularly in other societies. This constitutes a powerful argument for undertaking comparative studies and a warning against accepting generalizations which have been confirmed on a limited range of human beings. The avoidance of making unwarranted assumptions about "human nature" is not merely a matter of taking courses in psychology, but of being sensitive to other modes of existence in the way that some poets and dramatists are. If sociologists relied entirely upon statistical analysis and the logical manipulation of data they would create a great deal of information without being able to explain very much.

# BIBLIOGRAPHY

THE following selection of books is intended only as a guide to further reading, not as a comprehensive review of the literature. Some of the works relating to theory, method and special areas of study will inevitably present difficulties to the beginner and demand at least a basic grasp of sociology.

## 1. *Introductory Textbooks and Readings*

BOTTOMORE, T. *Sociology: A Guide to Problems and Literature.* London: George Allen & Unwin, 1962.

CHINOY, E. *Society: An Introduction to Sociology.* New York, Random House, 1961.

DAVIS, K. *Human Society.* New York, Macmillan, 1949.

GOULDNER, A. and GOULDNER, H. *Modern Sociology.* New York, Harcourt, Brace & World, 1963.

JOHNSON, H. *Sociology, A Systematic Introduction.* New York, Harcourt, Brace & Co., 1960.

MERTON, R. K., BROWN, L. and COTTRELL, L. Jr. (eds.) *Sociology Today: Problems and Prospects.* New York, Basic Books, 1959. (This book is intended for advanced students.)

## 2. *Methodology*

BRAITHWAITE, R. *Scientific Explanation.* London, Cambridge University Press, 1953.

COHEN, M. and NAGEL, E. *An Introduction to Logic and Scientific Method.* New York: Harcourt, Brace & World, 1936.

DURKHEIM, E. (CATLIN G., ed.) *The Rules of Sociological Method.* University of Chicago, 1938.

FISHER, R. *The Design of Experiments.* University of Edinburgh, 1949.

GIBSON, Q. *The Logic of Social Enquiry.* London, Routledge & Kegan Paul, 1960.

GREENWOOD, E. *Experimental Sociology.* New York, 1945.

MADGE, J. *The Tools of Social Science.* London, Longmans, Green, 1953.

NAGEL, E. *Structure of Science.* New York, Harcourt, Bruce & World, 1961.

SELLITZ, G., JAHODA, M., DEUTSCH, M. and COOK, S. *Research Methods in Social Relations.* New York, Holt & Co., 1959.

WEBER, M. (SHILS E. and FINCH H., trans.) *The Methodology of the Social Sciences.* Free Press, 1949.

147

## 3. *Theory and Concepts*

BECKER, H. and BARNES, H. *Social Thought from Lore to Science* (2nd ed.). Washington, D.C., Harren Press, 1952.

COSER, L. *The Functions of Social Conflict*. Free Press, 1965.

HOMANS, G. *The Human Group*. New York, Harcourt, Brace & World, 1950.

MERTON, R. K. *Social Theory and Social Structure* (rev. ed.). Free Press, 1957.

MILLS, C. W. *The Sociological Imagination*. New York, Oxford University Press, 1959. (There is a polemical intention underlying Mills's book which makes it enjoyable, but dangerous for the beginner.)

PARSONS, T., BALES, R. and SHILS, E. *Working Papers in the Theory of Action*. Free Press, 1953. (Presents difficulties to the beginner but constitutes a worthwhile intellectual challenge for the more ambitious student.)

SOROKIN, P. *Contemporary Sociological Theories*. New York, Harper, 1928. (The student should note that "contemporary" refers to the 1920's.)

## 4. *Social Change*

It is arguable that to treat social change as a special topic by giving it a separate heading is to obscure the fact that change is inherent in all social phenomena. Nonetheless, students of change have created a distinctive body of theoretical and empirical knowledge which demands special attention in a bibliography. The shortness of the list reflects not only our own shortage of space but also the relative lack of attention which social change has received in modern sociology.

MACIVER, R. and PAGE, C. *Society*, Book III. New York, Rinehart, 1949.

MOORE, W. *Social Change*. New Jersey, Prentice-Hall, 1963.

OGBURN, W. *Social Change with Respect to Culture and Original Nature*. New York, Viking, 1950.

SOROKIN, P. *Social and Cultural Dynamics* (1 vol. ed.). Boston: Sargent, 1957. (An ambitious attempt to trace patterns and rhythms of historical change, covering whole civilizations and utilizing data in every sphere of human activity.)

## 5. *Institutional Areas*

### (a) *Political*

ALMOND, G. and COLEMAN, J. (eds.) *The Politics of the Developing Areas*. Princeton University Press, 1960.

BUTLER, D. *The Study of Political Behaviour*. London, Hutchinson, 1958.

DUVERGER, M. *Political Parties*. New York, John Wiley, 1954.

ELAU, H. *Recent Developments in the Behavioural Study of Politics*. Stanford University Press, 1961.

HEBERLE, R. *Social Movements: An Introduction to Political Sociology*. New York, Appleton–Century–Crofts, 1951.

JANOWITZ, M. *The Military in the Political Development of New States*. University of Chicago, 1964.

LASSWELL, H. *Politics: Who Gets What, When, How*. New York, McGraw-Hill, 1936.

LIPSET, S. M. *Political Man*. New York, Doubleday, 1960.

LANE, R. *Political Life*. Free Press, 1959.

MACRIDIS, R. and BROWN, B. (eds.) *Comparative Politics: Notes and Readings*. Homewood, Dorsey, 1961.

NEUMANN, S. (ed.) *Modern Political Parties*. University of Chicago Press, 1956.

## (b) *Economic*

BENDIX, R. *Work and Authority in Industry*. New York, John Wiley, 1956.

CAPLOW, T. *The Sociology of Work*. University of Minneapolis, 1954.

FRIEDMANN, G. *Industrial Society*. Free Press, 1955.

HOSELITZ, B. and MOORE, W. (eds.) *Industrialization and Society*. Paris, UNESCO, 1963. (Concerned particularly with social change in the context of economic development.)

MOORE, W. *Industrial Relations and the Social Order* (rev. ed.). New York, Macmillan, 1951.

SMELSER, N. *The Sociology of Economic Life*. New Jersey, Prentice-Hall, 1963.

## (c) *Bureaucracy and Administration*

Research in this area is concerned particularly with political and economic organizations; we have given the titles under a separate heading because of the development of special theories and concepts in studying organizations.

BLAU, P. *Bureaucracy in Modern Society*. New York, Random House, 1956.

BLAU, P. *The Dynamics of Bureaucracy*. University of Chicago Press, 1955.

ETZIONI, A. *Complex Organizations: A Sociological Reader*. New York, Holt, Rinehard & Winston, 1961.

MERTON, R. *et al.* (eds.) *Reader in Bureaucracy*. Free Press, 1952.

SELZNICK, P. *Leadership in Administration*. Evanston, Peterson, 1958.

WEBER, M. (HENDERSON, L. and PARSONS, T., trans. and eds.) *The Theory of Social and Economic Organization*. New York, Oxford University Press, 1947.

## (d) *Marriage and the Family*

BOTT, E. *Family and Social Network*. London, Tavistock Publications, 1957.

GOODE, W. *The Family*. New Jersey, Prentice-Hall, 1964.

LEE, A. and LEE, E. *Marriage and the Family*. New York, Barnes & Noble, 1961. (An encyclopedic review of the area for the general reader with some knowledge of sociological jargon.)

MURDOCK, G. *Social Structure*. New York, Macmillan, 1949. (A comparative study of many types of society containing a wealth of material on kinship.)

## (e) *Social Stratification*

For further reading see the relevant sections of introductory textbooks.

BENDIX, R. and LIPSET, S. (eds.) *Class, Status and Power*. Free Press, 1953. (A wide-ranging collection of readings on social class and other forms of stratification.)

DAHRENDORF, R. *Class and Class Conflict in Industrial Society.* Stanford University Press, 1959.
Of special interest to the British reader are the following:
COLE, G. D. H. *Studies in Class Structure.* London, Routledge & Kegan Paul, 1955.
GLASS, D. V. (ed.) *Social Mobility in Britain.* London, Routledge & Kegan Paul, 1954.
STACEY, M. *Tradition and Change,* chaps 5, 6, and 8. Oxford University Press, 1960.
WILMOTT, P. and YOUNG, M. *Family and Class in a London Suburb.* London, Routledge & Kegan Paul, 1960.

## 6. The Individual in Society

This area of study is the special province of social psychology; two outstanding textbooks are:

LINDZEY, G. (ed.) *Handbook of Social Psychology.* Cambridge, Mass., Addison–Wesley, 1954.
MACCOBY, E., NEWCOMB, T. and HARTLEY E. (eds.) *Readings in Social Psychology.* New York, Holt, 1958.
Other works of special interest to the sociologist include:
ADORNO, T. W. *et al. The Authoritarian Personality.* New York, Harper, 1950. (This should be read in conjunction with R. Christie and M. Jahoda (eds.), *Studies in the Scope and Method of "The Authoritarian Personality",* Free Press, 1954.)
ELKIN, F. *The Child and Society: The Process of Socialization.* New York, Random House, 1960.
GERTH, H. and MILLS, C. *Character and Social Structure.* New York, Harcourt, Brace, 1953.
GOFFMAN, E. *The Presentation of the Self in Everyday Life.* University of Edinburgh Press, 1956.
LINTON, R. *The Cultural Background of Personality.* New York, Appleton–Century–Crofts, 1945.
MILLER, D. and SWANSON, G. *Inner Conflict and Defense.* New York, Holt & Co., 1960. (A sophisticated study of child-rearing practices and social behaviour as they vary amongst different sections of society.)
RIESMAN, D. *The Lonely Crowd* (abr.). New York, Doubleday, 1958. (Recent attempts to test Riesman's propositions concerning social conditions and personality types are collected together in, S. M. Lipset and L. Lowenthal (eds.), *Culture and Social Character,* Free Press, 1961.)

## 7. Applied Sociology

There exists a vast literature related to practical problems such as juvenile delinquency, racial prejudice, the planning of urban areas and industrial relations, but very little work on the direct application of social theory to social problems. Three recent books in this area are:

BENNIS, G., BENNE, K. and CHIN, R. *The Planning of Change: Readings in the Applied Behavioural Sciences.* New York, Holt & Co., 1961.

MERTON, R. and NISBET, R. (eds.) *Contemporary Social Problems.* New York, Harcourt, Brace & World, 1961.

WOOTTON, B. *Social Science and Social Pathology.* London, Allen & Unwin, 1959. (A review of the literature on applied social science, mainly concentrating on crime and delinquency in Britain.)

# INDEX

153